Bridging the Vernacular Gap

Bridging the Vernacular Gap

Safeguarding Devices in
English-Romanian Translation

Monica Augustina Zhekov

WIPF & STOCK · Eugene, Oregon

BRIDGING THE VERNACULAR GAP
Safeguarding Devices in English-Romanian Translation

Copyright © 2013 Monica Augustina Zhekov. All rights reserved. Except for brief quotations in critical publications or reviews, no part of this book may be reproduced in any manner without prior written permission from the publisher. Write: Permissions, Wipf and Stock Publishers, 199 W. 8th Ave., Suite 3, Eugene, OR 97401.

Wipf & Stock
An Imprint of Wipf and Stock Publishers
199 W. 8th Ave., Suite 3
Eugene, OR 97401

www.wipfandstock.com

ISBN 13: 978-1-62032-711-1

Manufactured in the U.S.A.

To my dearest husband Yordan

Contents

Abbreviations | x
Relevant Extracts for the Translation Devices | xi
Foreword by Silviu Rogobete | xiii
Introduction | xvii

1 Establishing the Methodology | 1
2 Constructing Suitable Imagery Device for Romanian | 3
   2.1 *Evaluating and Establishing the English Imagery Device as the Specific Element of the English Vernacular*
   2.2 *Toward Constructing the Most Suitable Device to Preserve and Transmit the English Imagery Element into Romanian*
   2.3 *Presentation of the Embodiment of the Imagery Element of English Vernacular through the Distinctiveness of Romanian Language of Young Adults*
3 Constructing Suitable Reported Language Device for Romanian | 20
   3.1 *Evaluating and Establishing the English Reported Language Device as the Specific Element of the English Vernacular*

- **3.2** *Toward Constructing the Most Suitable Device to Preserve and Transmit the English Reported Language Element into Romanian*
- **3.3** *Presentation of the Embodiment of the Reported Language Element of English Vernacular through the Distinctiveness of Romanian Language of Young Adults*

4 Constructing Suitable Facts and Data Device for Romanian | 29

- **4.1** *Evaluating and Establishing the English Facts and Data Device as the Specific Element of the English Vernacular*
- **4.2** *Toward Constructing the Most Suitable Device to Preserve and Transmit the Facts and Data Element into Romanian*
- **4.3** *Presentation of the Embodiment of the Facts and Data Element of English Vernacular through the Distinctiveness of Romanian Language of Young Adults*

5 Constructing Suitable Word Play Device for Romanian | 39

- **5.1** *Evaluating And Establishing The English Word Play Device As The Specific Element Of The English Vernacular*
- **5.2** *Toward Constructing the Most Suitable Word Play Device to Preserve and Transmit The Word Play Element into Romanian*
- **5.3** *Presentation of the Embodiment of the Word Play Element of English Vernacular through the Distinctiveness of Romanian Language of Young Adults*

6 Constructing Suitable Web Page Device for Romanian | 49

- **6.1** *Evaluating and Establishing the English Web Page Device as the Specific Element of the English Vernacular*
- **6.2** *Toward Constructing the Most Suitable Web Page Device to Preserve and Transmit the English Web Page Element into Romanian*

6.3 *Presentation of the Embodiment of the Web Page Element of English Vernacular through the Distinctiveness of Romanian Language of Young Adults*

7 Constructing Suitable Device for Integration of Foreign Language into Romanian | 62

7.1 *Evaluating and Establishing the Device for Integration of Foreign Language as the Specific Element of the English Vernacular*

7.2 *Toward Constructing the Most Suitable Device For Integration of Foreign Language to Preserve and Transmit the English Vernacular Element into Romanian*

7.3 *Presentation of the Embodiment of the Foreign Language Element of English Vernacular through the Distinctiveness of Romanian Language of Young Adults*

8 Evaluating the Functionality of the Designed Devices | 71

8.1 *Considerations of the New Tendencies Observed Among the Target Readership in Romania*

8.2 *The Efficiency of the Designed Language Devices in Preserving the English Vernacular*

Conclusion | 77

Appendices | 79

Questionnaire | 80

Bibliography | 85

Abbreviations

ST	Source Text
TT	Target Text
SL	Source Language
TL	Target Language
IT	Information Technology
Ro	Romanian
It	Italian

Relevant Extracts for the Translation Devices

1. Imagery device[1]
2. Reported language device[2]
3. Facts and data device[3]
4. Word play device[4]
5. Web page device[5]
6. Foreign language device[6]

---

1. Linda Newbery, Catcall (London: Orion Children's Books, 2006; reprint, 2007), 36.
2. Ibid., 124.
3. Ibid., 28.
4. Ibid., 51.
5. Ibid., 45.
6. Ibid., 44.

Foreword

THE PUBLICATION OF MONICA Zhekov is a welcomed applied research in the field of children literature in translation, in particular in the pursuit of preserving the distinctive cultural identity of the original in the translated text. The prominent characteristics of this exceptional academic work emerge through its successful intertwining of scientific material and a sensitive care for readership contexts.

In the recent years, many translated children and young adults books were made available to the Romanian readership, but how can one insure that the cultural elements of the original had been preserved and echoed into the translated work? The task of maintaining such elements in the translation may be considered even more difficult in children and young adult literature. That is because of the cultural gaps which the translator has to bridge and due to a mixture of genre used to stir up the interest of a rather rigorous young readership group.

Although the field of translating children literature offers general guidelines to the translators, there is not enough specific guidance offered in particular to the Romanian translators of this type of literature. Commenting on the rather low volume of translated Romanian books into other languages, Marino (1995) (*) points out that the inconsistent presence of Romanian contemporary literary criticism

Foreword

on the international scholarship stage was a contributory factor to the lack of awareness for a specific formulation of translation practice. Monica Zhekov's publication can be considered both an applied model of successful 'culture-transfer' into Romanian as well as a guide for translators of children literature into Romanian. This is particularly so since new features in the literary genre such as: web pages, word games, reconstruction of imageries, are in need to be properly dealt with.

Following a certain pattern for dealing with six main linguistic devices: imagery, reported language, facts and data, word play, web page and foreign language, Monica Zhekov begins by identifying each distinctive element of culture in the original Source Text. Thereafter, she proposes the most suitable technique to be used as a vehicle of transfer into the Target Text and ultimately she demonstrates the effective and inspired representation of each particular element into Romanian language. Lastly, her solutions are tested and proven operational by two distinct groups of her targeted readership.

Hence, Zhekov's publication is contributory to the field of translation study not only by setting an operational model for Romanian translators of children and young adult literature, but also by connecting translation theory and translation practice in a new and refreshing fashion. She positions the translator in a new role of custodian for the foreign elements as well as a responsible architect that recreates them in a different cultural context. Therefore, the transparency of the Source Text can be ensured as the Target Text is being mirrored to the reader by means of the linguistic devices that have been used, but without tampering with the substance of the original work. These influential characteristics of the present volume advance the academic research on the field to a new level of knowledge,

Foreword

accentuating profound theoretical grasp, scholarly creativity, and effective applicability.

*Adrian Marino, *Pentru Europa: Integrarea României; Aspecte Ideologice Și Culturale,* Colecția Plural (Iași: Polirom, 1995), 93.

Dr. Silviu Rogobete, Consul General of Romania and Dean of the Consular Corps of Cape Town, South Africa
Former Chancellor of the Faculty of Politics and Communication Sciences, West University of Timisoara, Romania

Introduction

THE GENERAL NORMS FOR translating children and young adult contemporary literature do not offer specific guidance to the Romanian translators to help them maintain and transmit the particularities of the English vernacular into Romanian. Even more, the lack of consistent presence of Romanian contemporary literary criticism on the international scholarship stage has failed to raise awareness for a specific formulation of translation practice.[7]

Without the benefits of specific practical assistance on how to tackle the postmodern English vernacular and how to implement it into Romanian, the translators of English contemporary literature for children and young adults into Romanian are left with no practical guidance and tools to help them complete the task successfully.[8] Therefore

---

7. Adrian Marino, *Pentru Europa: Integrarea României; Aspecte Ideologice și Culturale* [For Europe: The Integration of Romania; Ideological and Cultural Aspects], Colecția Plural (Iași: Polirom, 1995), 93. Stefanescu also affirms the deficient representation of indigenous Romanian literature for children which in his opinion was suppressed by translated books. D. Stefanescu, "Children's Literature in Romania: Between Despair and Hope," in *European Children's Literature II*, ed. P. Cotton (Kingston: Kingston University, 1998), 68.

8. It is my attempt to keep a balance between the usage of the source norms and the ones available in the target culture. For a more complete discussion on translation as a norm-governed activity see

Introduction

there is a real need for providing the translator with a suitable vehicle to help preservation and transmission of the unique vernacular into Romanian.[9] In order to facilitate the process of integrating the English original vernacular into Romanian I will attempt to identify significant devices which construct the unique vernacular of English young adults in *Catcall*[10] which is a recent[11] middle years'[12] fiction

---

Gideon Toury, *Descriptive Translation Studies and Beyond* (Philadelphia: John Benjamin Publishing Company, 1995), 57. The need for a fresh study in the area of translating children literature in order to develop new methodologies and tools is addressed in the section "Future Research in Translating for Children" in Eithne O'Connell, "Translating for Children," in *Word, Text, Translation: Liber Amicorum for Peter Newmark*, eds. Gunilla Anderman and Margaret Rogers (Clevedon: Multilingual Matters Ltd, 1999), 213.

9. The translators of children literature into Spanish, Swedish, Hebrew and other languages do benefit of practical directions like the ones offered by Isabel Pascua-Febles ["Translating Cultural References: The Language of Young People in Literary Texts," in *Children's Literature in Translation: Challenges and Strategies*, eds. Jan Van Coillie & Walter P. Verschueren (Manchester, UK: St. Jerome Publishing, 2006), 114], Riitta Oittinen [*Translating for Children*. Children's Literature and Culture, ed. Jack Zipes, v.11 (London: Garland Publishing, Inc., 2000), 74.], Tiina Puurtinen [*Linguistic Acceptability in Translated Children's Literature*. University of Joensuu Publications in the Humanities 15, ed. Sonja Tirkkonen-Condit (Joensuu: University of Joensuu, 1995), 51] and Zohar Shavit ["Translation of Children's Literature," in *The Translation of Children's Literature: A Reader*, ed. Gillian Lathey (Clevedon: Multilingual Matters Ltd, 2006), 26]. This in-depth guidance assists the translator on how to deal with cultural discrepancies but also with structural and linguistic matters.

10. Linda Newbery, *Catcall* (London: Orion Children's Books, 2006; reprint, 2007).

11. Catcall was first published in 2006.

12. The book is categorised as such in the author's website. *Catcall (Synopsis)*, [online], Available at http://www.lindanewbery.co.uk/midyearsfic.html, Accessed on 20 September 2007.

Introduction

book targeting young people of age 11–16[13] in the UK. The book is dealing with Jamie's strange behaviour in the midst of various changes in his family. The whole action in the book happens in the metropolitan city of London and nearby, places as High Wycombe, Metropolitan Line and M$_{25}$ are mentioned as locators[14]. In order to capture the readers' attention the book is scattered with drawings of lions, cats, legends and information about various cats, all part of what is called *Josh Book of Cats*. *Catcall* is what can be called a multi-meaning[15] title and the book's theme according to the author's statement was inspired by the author's encounter with the lion's gaze while visiting Cotswold Wildlife Park. The book itself is divided in 25 chapters each of them having representative titles in building the book as a unit, e.g. chapter 12: *Mask*, chapter 13: *Leo* and chapter 16: *Jungle*.

Romania is a new member of the European Union and visiting the UK becomes a feasible reality for the young readers. Hence the encounter of young Romanian people with the English context and life patterns through this book will benefit them in developing their understanding of cultural differences would they come across them in the future. Therefore this book might be considered as having an educational aspect for the young Romanian reader.

Analysing the ST of *Catcall* I will endeavour to construct these devices into Romanian and offer a presentation

---

13. International Baccalaureate Organization, *Middle Years Programme at a Glance: What is the Middle Years Programme?* [online], Available at http://www.ibo.org/myp/, Accessed on 12 December 2007.

14. L. Newbery, *Catcall*, 10.

15. The author herself reveals her affinity toward a one word title with more than one meaning. L. Newbery, *Catcall (website dedicated to the book)*, October 2006, updated May 2007 to include readers' contribution, [online], Available at http://www.lindanewbery.co.uk/catcall.html, Accessed on 20 September 2007.

Introduction

of their embodiment into the translation. It is expected that the incorporation of these devices will help to maintain the English vernacular while not diminishing the distinctiveness, presence and awareness that the translation needs to maintain in order to be suitable to the Romanian readership.

In the present work I will attempt to demonstrate that the unique English young adult vernacular in *Catcall* can be maintained and transmitted into the distinctive language of the targeted group of Romanian readers through implementing six translation devices which will serve as a vehicle of communicating this uniqueness. These devices that are going to be analysed are the imagery device, a reported language device, facts and data device, a word play device, a web page device and a device for integration of other foreign languages. By identifying and analysing the English vernacular devices in *Catcall* and reconstructing new ones into Romanian, the translators of English literature targeted for young adults will be provided with supporting tools to help them preserve and transmit the English vernacular into Romanian. Since the devices to be analysed cover specific variations of text and literary conventions met in English literature for young adults, the newly constructed devices will offer help to the translator in tackling difficult situations in translating this type of literature without losing the vernacular element during the translating process.

1

Establishing the Methodology

THE METHODOLOGY EMPLOYED FOR developing this dissertation includes three levels of research. First, I will analyse the difficulties and the particularities that each chosen device incorporates in its representation. In such a way I will establish the device as the specific element of the English vernacular that is to be reconstructed into the Romanian translation. To reconstruct the device I will address the issues of cultural suitability[1], semantic and structural implications. The representation of the embodiment of the English vernacular element through the distinctiveness of the Romanian language of young adults will demonstrate the development of the device and its efficiency and will be reflected into the achieved translation. Lastly, the function-

---

1. It is my understanding that the translators should first take into account the target readership. Then they should consider the position and function of the translation as well as the entire translating process including the form and strategies employed in achieving the translation which are altogether forming a complete process of connected facts. These facts are interdependent and reflect the relationship between function, product and process. This understanding is in line with Toury's comments about the translation within a target-oriented framework. G. Toury, *Descriptive Translation Studies and Beyond*, 24.

ality of the devices will be tested trough questioning a consistent number of 63 young Romanian readers by assessing their capacity to identify and comprehend the English vernacular element in two particular extracts which are going to be translated using the designed devices.[2] If these newly constructed devices prove to be successful in transmitting the English vernacular in the translation of *Catcall*, they will be suggested as potential tools for assisting the translators in preserving and implementing the English vernacular in other Romanian translations of English contemporary literature targeted for young adults.

---

2. The group consists of candidates of age between 11 and 16 from two different backgrounds: from a village called Damiş in Transylvania and Oradea, a city in Transylvania. The group selected is relevant being of the same age as the targeted readership in the UK.

2

Constructing Suitable Imagery Device for Romanian

2.1. Evaluating and Establishing the English Imagery Device as the Specific Element of the English Vernacular

IN ORDER TO DEAL with the difficulties to translate imageries in *Catcall*, I will first identify the ones whose incorporation into the Romanian language could not be successfully achieved without a reconstruction of the imagery which is represented into the original. Those imageries either do not have a direct correspondent in Romanian or due to the cultural and contextual considerations they could be misinterpreted by the reader if integrated without careful consideration of how the reader may visualise and understand that particular imagery.

Cohen brings in discussion the use of imagery in various disciplines such as mathematics taking into account that some people have reported little or no use of visual imagery while others make extensive use of visual imagery for problem solving. She also points out the importance of the writer's craft and ability to connect and to transfer to the reader's mind an image which has been constructed in the author's own mind.[1] Considering this view it seems that Newbery has got a good knowledge of her young reader's mind and was aware of the help she needed to offer to the young reader in order to make them understand a term from the banking field such as "bridging loan." Hence she decided to place the imagery in question which ought to be reconstructed in Romanian. The imagery of "bridge" may be encountered in other cultures and literary genres. However in this particular case to its basic structure is attached an economic dimension which is more frequently used in the developed countries such as the UK whose economies reflect the current changes in this economic climate.[2] Referring to the effect of the visual imageries Cohen acknowledges the processes involved in creating them, such as construction, modification and manipulation in order to fulfil the task.[3]

Due to the specific implications both in the ST cultural context and in its visual representation, I will select the above mentioned imagery of bridge as the most representative, whose syntactical structure and visual representation has to be modified in order to be transferred into TL without losing its vernacular element. Therefore the following extract presents the "bridge imagery" that is going to be recreated in the TL:

1. Gillian Cohen, "Visual Imagery in Thought," *New Literary History* 7/3, Thinking in the Arts, Sciences, and Literature (Spring 1976): 513–23, [online], Available at: http://www.jstor.org/stable/468560, Accessed on 05 July 2009.

2. Sarah Turner, *Economic Concerns Sap U.K. Stocks: Broker Downgrades Hit Real Estate and Travel-and-leisure Stocks*, [online], Available at http://www.marketwatch.com/story/economic-concerns-sap-uk-stocks-as-barclays-carnival-fallure stocks, Accessed on 13 July 2009.

3. G. Cohen, *Visual Imagery in Thought*, [online], 521.

Constructing Suitable Imagery Device for Romanian

'No, no, boys, it's not like that,' said Dad. 'It's not only my house, see—it's mine and Kim's. We've bought it together. She had to get a bridging loan.'

I imagined wads of banknotes like bricks, glued together in a huge arc, bridging the gap between Kim's house and Dad's.[4]

Another type of imagery to consider when translating *Catcall* into Romanian is the dreamed imagery which appears in Josh and Jamie's dreams. Its language also poses difficulties into transmitting the imagery into TL due to its deviations of form and structure. Referring to dream language Read suggests that the deviations and displacements are the result of the lack of rules concerning the form of such a language.[5]

The image of Splodge and Mister, Josh's family current and former cats, undergoes a series of changes through their transformation in size, colour, and acceptance of supernatural powers such as human abilities of speaking and of exercising authority over other beings.[6] Its presence in the dreams is shifting from a negative one, by keeping captive the baby sister and the mouse in Splodge's mouth, to a positive one, when Mister helps Josh and Jamie to face the ferocious lion.[7]

The purpose of this present study is to establish a method of how to deal with such devices, not to identify and analyse all of them. Therefore I will make use of the

---

4. L. Newbery, *Catcall*, 36.

5. Allen Walker Read, "Dreamed Words: Their Implications for Linguistic Theory," *American Speech* 44/2 (May 1969): 118–28, [online], Available at http://www.jstor.org/stable/455101, Accessed on 5 July 2009.

6. L. Newbery, *Catcall*, 133–35 and 165–67.

7. Ibid., 133–35.

most illustrative examples presented in its English context. That is the "bridging loan imagery."

2.2. Toward Constructing the Most Suitable Device to Preserve and Transmit the English Imagery Element into Romanian

The central problematic with translating the "bridging loan" imagery into Romanian is not its usage in the economic field but the different visual effect that it represents for the Romanian readership. In the SL the imagery of "bridge" includes in its meaning the existence of bricks and the geometrical shape of a huge arc.[8] The Romanian economic correspondent of "bridging loan" is "credit punte." The imagery of this term is defined by *punte* which can be translated as "footbridge." Its structure is of a flexible design of an upside down bridge with a different orientation of the planks, constructed in a usually parallel fashion and from wooden material.

Having established that "bridging loan" in the above extract represents the English vernacular, its transmission into the TL is essential and therefore I will attempt to maintain its intended economic dimension. In order to identify its presence in the Romanian language I will refer to its collocation in the Romanian economic field correspondent to the British one.

Searching *The British National Corpus* and *Google Search Engine* I found out that "creditul punte"[9] is the Ro-

---

8. Ibid., 36.

9. The term is always used in the finance and banking field. A search for this term in the British National Corpus has generated 36 solutions. British National Corpus, [online], Available at http://sara.natcorp.ox.ac.uk/cgi-bin/saraWeb?qy=bridging+loan&mysubmit=Go, Accessed on 20 May 2009. In the Romanian context the usage of its correspondent "credit punte" is mainly used in relation to exchanging

manian equivalent which represents the same economic value as the "bridging loan." The problematic which results from the decision to use "creditul punte" is linked with the representation of different imagery into Romanian. Therefore I will have to evaluate it and decide whether I will construct the imagery based on the term "footbridge," the nearest translation of the Romanian "punte," or whether I should change the representation of the imagery employing in Romanian the term *pod* "bridge." Constructing the imagery around the word *pod* "bridge" will bring in discussion further implications such as the non-existence of *creditul pod* in the economic sector in Romania. This term can be translated into English as "bridging loan" but such a choice will be redundant and would fail to represent its economic value as intended in the original text.

Searching for the term *punte* "footbridge" on the *Corpuseye*[10], a project of Syddansk University in Denmark which contains approximately 21.4 million Romanian words from the Business Sector, I was provided with 70 results from which nine contained the term *creditul punte* in its financial usage as a "financial loan." In order to establish the collocates for *punte* "footbridge" I will follow up to a certain degree the model employed by Knowles and Malmkjaer in their study on collocation where they searched for the concordance lines for the node *dragon* in *Jane and the Dragon* and *The Dragon's Purpose* by Baynton.[11] I have searched in the *Corpuseye* corpus taking *punte* as the node and below I

one's property for another property or for buying a new property. *Credit Punte BCR* [Bridging Loan BCR], [online], Available at http://www.cauta-imobiliare.ro/articole/credit-punte-extra-bcr.html, Accessed on 20 May 2009.

10. *Corpuseye: Romanian Business Corpus*, [online], Available at http://corp.hum.sdu.dk/cqp.ro.html, Accessed on 20 May 2009.

11. Murray Knowles and Kirsten Malmkjaer, *Language and Control in Children's Literature* (London: Routledge, 1996), 71.

will present the outcome of this study expressed as sets of concordance lines with about four words on each side of the node, where possible. The words on each side of the node are also identified as left or right context, depending of their distribution on either side of the node. Below are supplied the nine instances that contained the aforementioned node. The node is represented in the middle column. For reader's convenience I have supplied the English translation of each line underneath each instance.

Table 1. Search of the concordance lines for punte on Corpuseye: Romanian Business Corpus which generated nine instances that contained creditul punte "the bridging loan"[12]

1	pentru nevoi personale,	creditul punte	Depozitul și Creditul
	for personal needs,	the bridging loan	*the savings and the loan*
2	descoperire de cont.	credit punte	și credit ipotecar;
	overdraft.	Bridging loan	*and mortgage*
3		Creditul punte	poate constitui avansul creditului pentru locuință
		The bridging loan	*can be considered as an advance payment for the new home*
4	la creditele imobiliare	(creditul punte;	
	regarding the construction loan	(the bridging loan;	
5	care a lansat	creditul punte	și apoi pachetul Confort

12. *Corpuseye: Romanian Business Corpus*, [online].

Constructing Suitable Imagery Device for Romanian

	who launched	the bridging loan	*and after that the Confort Pack*
6	a două credite,	creditul punte	Poate deveni avansul pentru un alt
	of two loans,	the bridging loan	*can become the initial payment for another*
7	și	creditul punte	de la Banca Reglementelor Internaționale
	and	the bridging loan	*from the Bank for International Settlements*
8	și	creditele punte	(bridge) de la Banca
	and	the bridging loan	*(bridge) from the Bank*
9		creditele punte	de la BRI, bănci străine, guverne
		the bridging loans	*from BIS, foreign banks, governments*

Other concordance lines of the same search give strong indication of *punte* "footbridge" being used as an imaginary link or relationship achieved between different objects, persons and locations as indicated in the following table. For reader's convenience the Romanian translation of each line is supplied underneath each instance. From the following table it is clear that *punte* "bridge" is very often used to create an imaginary link between objects, persons and countries. This observation leads to a conclusion that it is very appropriate to use the term in this form for representing the bridge imagery in the relevant example provided for the task of constructing a suitable device for transmitting the difficult to translate imagery into Romanian. Some examples of the linking relationships achieved by *punte* "bridge" in the table below are the followings: bridge toward other countries, *punte de legătură spre alte țări*, a network for exchange, *punte de legătură pentru schimburi* and bridge between the East and the West, *punte de legătură între Est și Vest*. One can notice that in Romanian *punte* "footbridge" often collocates with *de legătură* which depending on the context can be translated as "a bridge," "a link," "contact" or "continuity" where all of these incorporate the implication of connectivity or achieved relationship between objects, persons or locations.

Table 2. Concordance lines for "punte" indicating that the term can be used as an imaginary link between objects, persons and locations.

1	America rămâne o	Punte	de legătură spre alte țări
	America continues to be a	Bridge	toward other countries
2	rușii au nevoie de o	Punte	de legătură pentru schimburi
	The Russians need to build a	Network	for exchange
3	Europa de Est ca o	Punte	de legătură cu vestul continentului
	Eastern Europe is a	Link	to the western part of the continent
4	să construim un fel de	Punte	de legătură între ce
	to build a sort of	Bridge	between that
5	un mod de a construi o	Punte	de legătură între absolvirea școlii

Constructing Suitable Imagery Device for Romanian

	a way to achieve a	Continuity	after graduating the school
6	am acționat ca o	Punte	de legătură între Est și Vest
	we have acted as a	Bridge	between the East and the West
7	intenția de a stabili o	Punte	de legătură directă între cititori
	the intention to establish a direct	Contact	among the readers
8	intenția de a stabili o	Punte	de legătură directă între cerere
	the intention to establish a direct	Link	between the demand and

From a study of the right context of "punte," which are the words on the right column of "punte" in the *Romanian Bussiness Corpora*[13], one can notice that the most frequent linking words with the other part of the sentence are *între* "between" and *de* "of." Both of these represent the relationship or the connection achieved by *punte* "footbridge." Looking at the frequency of *între* "between" in the *Romanian Business Corpus* on *Corpuseye*[14] there are six occurrences in the above mentioned search having *punte* as the node for the collocation. A relatively high frequency is observed in regard to *de* "of," 20 in total. Besides the number of frequencies in the table below indicated by number [num], the reader can also notice the frequency distribution list (freq) and the relative frequencies list (rel) indicated with *italic* characters.

13. Ibid.
14. Ibid.

Table 3. Frequency distribution list of linking words occurring on the right side of punte in Compuseye[15] Corpus

ROM_BUSINESS (70)			
frequencies:	*rel*	freq	*num*
de	6392	28.6	[20]
,	1164	10.1	[7]
între	73469387	8.6	[6]
"	32653061	5.8	[4]
pentru	891	4.3	[3]
către	6752	4.3	[3]
specială	2551.02	2.9	[2]
;	60.24	2.9	[2]
poate	95.18	2.9	[2]
spre	199.82	2.9	[2]
ca	30.76	2.9	[2]
și	163265.3	2.9	[2]
semiindependentă	20408.16	1.5	[1]
motrice	10204.08	1.5	[1]
acordat	73.41	1.5	[1]
procentuale	425.17	1.5	[1]
comună	206.14	1.5	[1]
spate	192.52	1.5	[1]
inclusiv	40.89	1.5	[1]
prea	31.93	1.5	[1]
(	2.89	1.5	[1]
"	20408.16	1.5	[1]
spre	24.97	1.5	[1]
față	9.9	1.5	[1]

15. Ibid.

Constructing Suitable Imagery Device for Romanian

pentru	0.99	1.5	[1]
o	1.59	1.5	[1]
.	0.21	1.5	[1]

Observing the left side of "punte" in the *Romanian Bussiness Corpora*[16], one can notice that the most frequent linking words with the other part of the sentence are *o* "a" or "an," in total 28 instances.

Table 4. Frequency distribution list of linking words occurring on the left side of punte in the Corpuseye[17] Corpus

ROM_BUSINESS (70)			
frequencies:	*rel*	freq	*num*
o	124970	40.1	[28]
creditul	468077	7.2	[5]
pe	2745	7.2	[5]
de	255	5.8	[4]
creditele	148123	4.3	[3]
și	18367346	4.3	[3]
,	213	4.3	[3]
O	119.6	2.9	[2]
Y212	20408.16	1.5	[1]
X176	20408.16	1.5	[1]
5,4	2040.81	1.5	[1]
imobiliar	43.42	1.5	[1]
singură	188.96	1.5	[1]
credit	12.86	1.5	[1]
împrumuturile	20408.16	1.5	[1]

16. Ibid.
17. Ibid.

inferior	443.65	1.5	[1]
acum	12.16	1.5	[1]
sub	17.73	1.5	[1]
"	20408.16	1.5	[1]
ca	3.84	1.5	[1]
cu	0.91	1.5	[1]
în	20408.16	1.5	[1]
-	816.32	1.5	[1]
de	0.15	1.5	[1]
¤	0.51	1.5	[1]

Baker acknowledges that when dealing with collocations, the translators are placed in a position of resolving the tension between accuracy and naturalness. They are searching for the group of words in the TL which will communicate the message in such a way that is representative for the reader, with the least possible deviation from the words' meaning in the SL.[18]

Establishing the appropriate correspondent of the "bridging loan" as *creditul punte* I will have to assess whether the newly created imagery will suppress the English vernacular element as represented in the original. The fragile material structure of the "footbridge" incorporated in the meaning of *punte* is stripped off the solid and stable characteristics of the English "bridge." Nevertheless it will still maintain its purpose to connect the two objects (in this case Dad's house and Kim's) and offer a rational aid as intended in the ST. Therefore, I believe that using *credit punte* is the best choice in order to implement the vernacular imagery into Romanian since the economic field in Romania

---

18. Mona Baker, *In Other Words: A Coursebook on Translation* (London: Routledge, 1992; reprint, 1994 and 1995), 56.

Constructing Suitable Imagery Device for Romanian

has already adopted the term *credit punte*[19] "bridging loan." Furthermore the above explained imagery constructed on the image of *punte* "footbridge" does transfer the same idea of relationship and connectivity between the objects as the "bridging loan" in the ST. There are some variations of directions and structure in the imagery as explained above but these do not distort the initial intention of the author, that of offering a mental-visual aid to the young reader.

2.3. Presentation of the Embodiment of the Imagery Element of English Vernacular through the Distinctiveness of Romanian Language of Young Adults

In the form that "bridging loan" is represented in my Romanian translation, the vernacular element is maintained at the highest degree. Maintaining the "bricks" *cărămizile* as the imagery substance for the "footbridge," the possibly implied fragile and unsteady construction of the *punte*[20] "footbridge," usually constructed of a light and flexible structure, is eliminated. The term "punte" is toughened by collocating with stronger lexical elements which determine its strength,

---

19. Cristina Ungureanu, Financial Analyst of FinZoom, defines *creditul punte* "*bridging loan*" as "the loan given for a short or medium term and which is granted to the eligible customers who have a property (flat or house) which they intent to sell." Cristina Ungureanu, *Creditul Punte* [Bridging Loan], [online], Available at http://www.finzoom.ro/Info/art/Advices/Creditul-PUNTE~1dcfdcda87b5467cac5ca9d67e2afa94/, Accessed on 13 July 2009.

20. Ana Zecheru provides the following definition: "Narrow footbridge often made of a wooden plank or a beam laid over a ditch, a slope or over the waters." Ana Zecheru, "Punte" [Footbridge], in *DEX online: Dicționare explicative ale limbii române* [DEX online: Explanatory Dictionaries of the Romanian Language], [online], Available at http://dexonline.ro/search.php?cuv=punte, Accessed on 13 July 2009.

namely, "cǎramizile." Another element of strength here is "linked" *lipite* which demonstrates the connection between bricks and thus adds to the imagery strength and as a result compensates for the initial image of a fragile footbridge.

Therefore the imagery represented brings into the mind of the young reader a slight variation of the traditional term "footbridge" *punte* but with no distortion of its relevance and validity in the financial field. The added strength in the imagery is represented by *bricks* and *link* instead of wooden planks, the usual material of a footbridge in the Romanian cultural context. The present translator has made this choice in order to maintain the solid bridge representation identified in the ST and not to allow the visually frail image of a common Romanian footbridge to take over the young reader's mind. The following illustrations compare both imageries. Illustration 1 represents the "bridge" imagery which the author reflects on the young reader's mind as a visual aid to understand the financial term "bridging loan" and illustration 2 represents the "footbridge" *punte* imagery based on the translator's choice to reconstruct the "bridge" in the TL.[21]

Illustration 1: "The bridge" imagery constructed by the author in the ST.

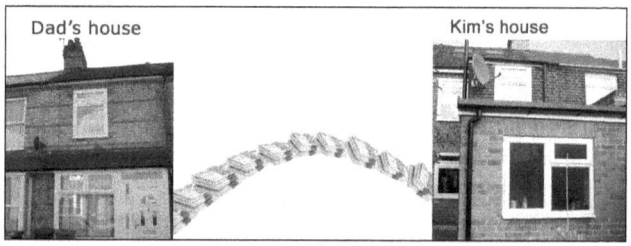

One can observe that the representation of the "bridge" imagery in the ST embodies the arch shape, and

21. Illustrations 1 and 2 were designed by the author of this present research.

Constructing Suitable Imagery Device for Romanian

the wads are partly overlapping, while in the TL the shape of the "footbridge" represents the shape and structure of a "Romanian footbridge." In this case the planks, which are represented by "wads of banknotes like bricks" are laid parallel to each other without overlapping.[22]

Illustration 2. Representation of the "footbridge" *punte* **imagery constructed by the translator in the TL.**

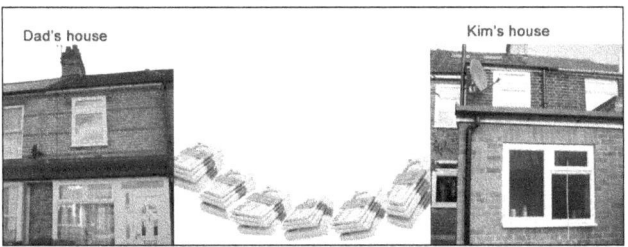

Toward a better representation of the linking structure between these "wads of banknotes as bricks" the translator maintains in the TL the same process involved in the SL and represents these wads of banknotes as being "glued together" *lipite împreună*. However, making her choice to represent "footbridge" *punte* imagery, the translator does not have any longer the option to continue with building the last part of the imagery in the same fashion as in the ST, namely, in the form of "a huge arc." As previously explained, the Romanian footbridge imagery can only be represented as an upside down arc resembling to a "U" shape rather than an arc. For that reason I have translated the "huge arc" as *punte uriașă* "a huge footbridge." By implementing this choice I have successfully maintained the standard image of the Romanian footbridge throughout the process of reconstructing the bridge imagery for the Romanian young

---

22. The reader should tolerate the imperfect representation of the parallelism between the wads of banknotes which is subject to the editing limitations.

reader, without dropping the specific element which the author had constructed as an aid for the English young reader. Even more, I have succeeded to transmit into Romanian the financial element integrated by the author through the "bridging loan" without creating any tension between this term and its financial correspondent in Romanian *creditul punte*. Analysing the Romanian terminology used in the financial field and taking in consideration the Romanian cultural element, I have constructed a bridging relationship between the imagery in the ST and the one in the TL. The process of reconstructing was focused on maintaining the English specific element "wads of banknotes as bricks" which I have successfully incorporated in the structure of the Romanian footbridge *punte*. Such an integration of a rather unusual structural element in the composition of "footbridge" indicates to the Romanian young reader that its role is to provide a visual aid for the intended image representing the linking relationship which Josh's Dad had underlined in his discussion with Josh.

In conclusion, the transformation of the "bridge" imagery from the ST in the TL is built by the translator taking into consideration the relevant cultural issues and implications from both the UK cultural context and the Romanian one. Even more, the findings from the collocation study having the node *punte* "footbridge" in *The Romanian Business Corpus* have confirmed translator's decision to use *punte* "footbridge" as a substitute for "bridge." After analysing the concordance lines for the node *punte* "footbridge" it has been concluded that the "footbridge" *punte* within its left and right contexts indicates and confirms the idea of relationship as the linking element intended by the author in the ST. Therefore the presentation of the "bridging loan" through *creditul punte* is clearly illustrated in Romanian as presented below:

Constructing Suitable Imagery Device for Romanian

"Nu, nu, băieți, nu-i așa," zise tata. "Vedeți, nu-i numai casa mea—ea a mea și a Kimei. Am cumpărat-o împreună. Ea a trebuit să obțină un credit punte."

Îmi imaginam teancuri de bancnote precum cărămizile, lipite împreună într-o punte uriașă, acoperind distanța dintre casa Kimei și cea a tatei.

3

Constructing Suitable Reported Language Device For Romanian

3.1. Evaluating and Establishing the English Reported Language Device as the Specific Element of the English Vernacular

IN ORDER TO DEAL with the issue of translating the reported language in *Catcall*, I will first identify the particular instances of reported language whose incorporation into Romanian language could cause some difficulties for the targeted reader. Translation of these occurrences would require upholding of the vernacular particularities of the English reported speech specific to the English young readers while maintaining a register suitable and acceptable for the targeted readership.

Baker advises that contextually defined register serving the needs of the targeted readership is the translator's solution for dealing with the particularity of the situationally defined language. The TT should respond to the anticipated terminology by the native speaker related to the nature of the contextual framework. Diversions from the acceptable use of communicative devices limited to the given context can only be allowed on intentionally formulated grounds with the purpose of underlining the cultural elements of the source language.[1]

Another important issue for the translator to consider is the children's comprehension of literary textual elements with various levels of complexity. The field has been researched in regard to children's "awareness of fiction, the ability to generalise and abstract, understanding of the use of indirect speech, the reconstruction of viewpoints and feelings, and the development of moral understanding."[2] The results have provided knowledge but not to the extent to cover children's ability on different stages of development. Further studies have shown the connection between children abilities gained from their exposure to multimedia and the use of these abilities for comprehension of literary texts.[3]

The impressive, detailed reported speech of unhappy events, as being told off by one's teacher are seen in the British culture as a way of gaining popularity among other pupils. This may not yet be the case in the Romanian context where disclosure of such detailed information could bring shame and inhibition to the speaker. Nevertheless, it may be argued that in order to maintain the English vernacular in such a reported speech the Romanian young reader should be exposed to the attitude of the English character so that they may get acquainted with the culturally contextual approach of the book context.

1. M. Baker, *In Other Words: A Coursebook on Translation*, 16.

2. Emer O'Sullivan, *Comparative Children's Literature*, trans. Anthea Bell (London: Routledge, 2005), 92.

3. Ibid., 92, 93.

Monica Augustina Zhekov

After analysing the ST it was found that the most illustrative example of reported speech presented in a rather unusual format to the common one found in similar genres in TL is Josh's account of the events involved in the process of being told off by his teacher. This encounter is vividly represented in the following extract:[4]

> Result: mega ear-bashing from Rick, along with a lot of head-shaking, and *utter disgrace*, and *shocked to hear of such behaviour*, and a threat to phone our parents if anything like this ever happened again, *and* a lunchtime detention for both of us. This took up the whole of break, so we were late for History, and had to explain to Mrs Cartwright, while Bex sniggered.[5]

Referring to such translation difficulties as those mentioned earlier Aixela underlines that cultural diversity formulated through the specific behavioural, moral, analytical and other elements of different linguistic communities presents grounds for variations which necessitate the translator's particular attention.[6] The problematic element in this particular example is the form in which the reported speech is introduced, without any preliminary warning that such an abrupt speech is going to follow. Another problem posing element can be considered the harsh register used in the ST such as "utter disgrace" and "mega ear-bashing" which necessitates the translator's decision on whether this could be accepted by the Romanian readership. In particular "mega ear-bashing" poses

---

4. L. Newbery, *Catcall*, 124.

5. Ibid.

6. Javier Franco Aixela, "Culture-Specific Items in Translation," in *Translation, Power, Subversion*, eds. Roman Alvarez and M. Carmen-Africa Vidal, *Topics in Translation* 8, eds. Susan Bassnett and André Lefevere (Clevedon, UK: Multilingual Matters Ltd, 1996), 53.

difficulties in its translation into Romanian. The important place of the term "mega" in the ST is acknowledged but its transformation into the TL is characterised by the difficulty of linking the term with a suitable Romanian word. Therefore in this situation the translator will follow Baker's recommendation who underlines that diversion of grammatical compositions between the source and target texts necessitates the provision of additional informative wording in order to provide continuity of the meaning between the two texts.[7]

3.2. Toward Constructing the Most Suitable Device to Preserve and Transmit the English Reported Language Element into Romanian

To efficiently reconstruct the reported language device into Romanian I will take in consideration the expectations of the young Romanian readership, the norms in the TL, the emphasis of the author and the way she constructed the humorous effect in the ST. A successful achievement of the process would benefit from guidance related to particularities of Halliday's model articulated in his analysis of the subject-object relationship in a statement.[8] Compared to Halliday's model[9] in which he makes distinction between the grammatical subject, psychological subject and logical subject, my study will incorporate variations of these categories. A specific attention should be given to the difficulty in translating of cultural specific items such as "ear-bashing" mentioned in the previous

---

7. M. Baker, *In Other Words: A Coursebook on Translation*, 86.

8. M. A. K. Halliday and C. M. I. M. Matthiessen, *An Introduction to Functional Grammar*, 3rd ed., (London: Arnold, 2004), 57.

9. Ibid., 57.

example which should be reconstructed in the TL without encountering essential loss of the cultural particularities. In line with Aixela, by cultural specific item I understand a language unit loaded with unique culturally defined meaning which creates discontinuity between the source and the target texts transpired due to lack of corresponding terminology.[10]

In my example of reported speech I will analyse the following instance which differs considerably in format and structure in other similar TL texts: "Result: mega ear-bashing from Rick, along with a lot of head-shaking, and *utter disgrace*, and *shocked to hear of such behaviour*, and a threat to phone our parents if anything like this ever happened again, *and* a lunchtime detention for both of us."[11]

Concerning the structure, the above mentioned example has little in common with the example offered by Halliday, namely, "This teapot my aunt was given by the duke."[12] However, in both instances one can identify the presence of an actor, a subject and a theme. In my example, "result" is the subject to which "ear-bashing" + "head-shaking" + "utter disgrace" + "shocked of such behaviour" + "a threat to phone" + (and) "a lunchtime detention" are all attached and incorporated into the actual "result." This subject according to Halliday can also be considered as the theme leading to the understanding that these two are combined in one element. In my example the actor is "Rick" who performs the actions; what is clearly missing here is the verb in the simple past form "was" which in this particular case the author has replaced with colon (:) for additional impact. The threatening action presented

---

10. J. F. Aixela, *Culture-Specific Items in Translation*, 57.

11. L. Newbery, *Catcall*, 124.

12. M. A. K. Halliday and C. M. I. M. Matthiessen, *An Introduction to Functional Grammar*, 57.

with the phrase "to phone our parents" is introduced by the conditional clause "if anything like this ever happened again." The fulfilment or lack of fulfilment of this condition will determine whether "our parents" will become or not "the object" of Rick's intended action.

As one can notice, the structure of the above example is quite complex in English. The translation of the example into the TL will be established on two substantial decisions. On the one hand, the translator should consider to comply with the TL grammatical norms concerning the sentences' structure and the relationship subject—object. On the other hand, the translator should decide to what degree the English vernacular element will be represented into the TL.

3.3. Presentation of the Embodiment of the Reported Language Element of English Vernacular through the Distinctiveness of Romanian Language of Young Adults

The format of the reported speech in the example supplied presents an abrupt structure which is not usually met in the Romanian books written for children and young adults. However, this representation of reported speech that aims to reflect the attitude of a teenager in the UK is valuable for the Romanian readership who will try to build a picture of Josh, the English character that reports the incident.[13] The Romanian reader should not be restricted

13. In my attempt to reconstruct the English vernacular present in the particular excerpts, I will follow Isabel Pascua-Febles' advice to the translator of young adults' literature not to focus only on the structure of the ST but also to consider, at the same degree, the place that the particular work occupies in the source culture. I. Pascua-Febles, *Translating Cultural References: The Language of Young People in Literary Texts*, 114.

Monica Augustina Zhekov

from having access to the image of Josh as constructed by the author through her ideology. This may come in conflict with the general ideology which the current native books for children try to build in the mind of the young Romanian reader. I agree with Hunt that books impact their readers. Ideological influence is part of this impact. The difference between adult and children literature appears to be in the provision of assumed text assessment capacity which is lacking to the children readers. Texts convey authors' message which possesses the potential to instruct, educate, reveal cultural values, influence and even manipulate the readers. The children literature has all these characteristics but due to its nature of serving its readers in the critical process, its manipulative capacity is further empowered. Hence children texts carry ideologies and influence their readers in this aspect. This calls for authors' awareness and care of the impact of their writings by making the texts' cultural values more accessible to their readers.[14]

For achieving a suitable translation of the given example, I have preserved the abrupt and unexpected introduction of the subject, "Result" *Rezultatul*, but additionally I have added the definite article represented by the particle "l." In this way, I have translated "mega ear-bashing" as *surzirea urechilor la maxim* so that I could maintain the trend of "mega"[15] which due to my choice of *maxim* also incorporates the meaning of "great, large and brilliant."

The gloss translation into English of my choice for "mega ear-bashing" is represented below. The gloss

---

14. Peter Hunt, *An Introduction to Children's Literature* (Oxford: Oxford University Press, 1994), 3.

15. "Mega," in *Oxford Talking Dictionary*. CD-ROM. Learning Company Properties Inc., 1998.

translation is indicated by GLOSS, my translation by M and the ST by O.

M: Rezultatul: surzirea urechilor la maxim de către Rick

GLOSS: The result: maximum ear deafness achieved by Rick

O: Result: mega ear-bashing from Rick

Opting for this choice, I have successfully maintained the ST intensity and the element of surprise in the translated reported speech, adding additional clarity in reference to the actor performing the action (Rick) through the use of the particular indicator *de către* "by." The subject in the TL is maintained as in the ST, namely "Result" is translated as *Rezultatul*. Maintaining the condition *dacă* "if," the object of Rick's intended action relies again on the fulfilment of the aforementioned condition.

Below is offered the translation of the reported speech provided as an example in the beginning of this chapter. The translator has also emphasised the emotionally loaded words as in the ST by representing them in italics. These are *rușine totală* "utter disgrace," *sunt șocat să aud de un asemenea comportament* "shocked to hear of such behaviour" and *și* "and."

> Și, desigur, acela fuse momentul în care Domnul O'Shea deshisese ușa. Încremenise, se uitase la mine, și ne spusese la amândoi să mergem înăuntru.
>
> Rezultatul: surzirea urechilor la maxim de către Rick, împreună cu clătinări dezaprobatoare din cap, și *rușine totală*, și *sunt șocat să aud de un asemenea comportament*, și o amenințare cu sunatul părinților dacă ceva de genul acesta se va întâmpla din nou, *și* reținere în clasă pentru amândoi în timpul pauzei de masă. Aceasta a ținut toată pauza, așa că întârziaserăm la ora

> de istorie, așa că trebuiserăm să dăm explicații
> Doamnei Cartwright în timp ce Bex chichotise.

In line with Lukens, I agree that humoristic occurrences in children's literature contribute to the positive acceptance of the text by its readers. The fun brought to the young readers is usually situational established on the unusual development of events.[16] This is clearly the case with the present example when seen in its context.

---

16. Rebecca J. Lukens, *A Critical Handbook of Children's Literature*, 6th ed. (Harlow, England: Longman, 1999), 220.

4

Constructing Suitable Facts and Data Device for Romanian

4.1. Evaluating and Establishing the English Facts and Data Device as the Specific Element of the English Vernacular

AT THE CENTRE OF this chapter is the facts and data device. Its nature as related to the present book is complex, incorporating images, exhibiting particular handwriting style, dealing with Latin terms and inclusive of metafictional and humoristic elements. In English as well as in other European languages, the use of Latin is very common in scientific texts.[1] In the present book the use of Latin in contrast with the English register is used to enhance the humoristic effect of the text on its readers. Newbery uses Latin names

---

1. Sala presents a summary list of the animal names that are common in the Romance languages (Romanian, Italian, Spanish and Portuguese) with particular emphasis on the similarities between the Romanian and Latin names of the animals. Marius Sala, "The History of Words: Latin Animal Names," *Pro Saeculum* 7–8 (2006): 25.

for animals as in: *felidae* /cat family, *turdus viscivorus*/ mistle thrush, *bombus bombus*/ bumble bee and *troglodytes troglodytes*/wren. The humoristic effect works very well in English by the difference in the registers between the two languages as well as by the association that the reader can make when reading the Latin names. Even more, the humoristic effect of such contrasting comparisons is pointed out by Josh's opinion in relation to *troglodytes troglodytes*/ wren—"Big name for a very small bird."[2]

McLcish underlines very well the role of the translator in the process of translating comedy specific to the source context. This process requires more proactive dealings with the text than working with other literary texts. The result from the translation is not only conversion of the message from the ST into the TT and for the target audience but also to preserve the humour of the original into the translation and make it available to the readers. Hence the transformation of the text places the burden on the translator to reveal the comedy of the text, its content and register to the target readers within their own context. While this requires the translator's active engagement with the texts specific elements, some comedy texts may not need to undergo much change in order to achieve their purpose in the TT and audience.[3]

As it has been mentioned previously, the English language maintains the humoristic effect based on the Latin use due to the difference in the registers between the two languages. However, this is not the case with the Romanian language which due to its general Latin character[4] shares

2. L. Newbery, *Catcall*, 28.

3. Kenneth McLeish, "Translating Comedy," in *Stages of Translation*, ed. David Johnston (Bristol: The Longdunn Press Ltd., 1996), 154, 155.

4. For a complete discussion on the Latin based vocabulary

Constructing Suitable Facts and Data Device for Romanian

close similarities in the animal names with the Latin. Hence the humorous effect in the TL might have to be constructed using the similarities between the two languages rather than the contrast between them. In such a way it can also constitute a learning device for the young reader who encounters these scientific names in the school textbooks.[5] The translator will have to take such factors in consideration before tackling the specific elements of the texts. The complexity of the translation is further intensified with the fact that the Latin terminology is represented together with the drawings of wild cats. Both these elements along with the particularities of the handwriting style are part of *Josh's Book of Cats* and as such can be considered a specific language device which is loaded with the cultural element marked by particularities of Josh's style and personality transposed on the page of his *Book of Cats*.[6]

The combination of image and text empowers further the communication of the message to its intended readers. The present author implements this influential communicator of message relying on the readers' interpretive skills through visual means. Captured by the power of the image

---

of Romanian see Alexandru Rosetti, *Istoria limbii române: Limbile slave meridionale* [The History of Romanian Language: The Slavic Meridional Languages], vol.3, sec.VI-XII (București: Editura Științifică; Ediția a 5-a revizuită și adăugită, 1964), 27.

5. Referring to the Latin character of the Romanian language the authors of *Limba Română: Manual pentru clasele a IX-a și a X-a* [Romanian Language: Handbook for the 1st and 2nd Year High School Pupils] maintain that due to this Latin character most of the recent neologisms in Romanian were borrowed from other Romance languages also based on Latin or from the Latin language itself. Elena Berea-Găgeanu, Doina Moigrădeanu, Florin D. Popescu și Cezar Tabarcea, *Limba Română: Manual pentru clasele a IX-a și a X-a* [Romanian Language: Handbook for the 1st and 2nd Year Secondary School Pupils] (București: Editura Didactică și Pedagogică, R.A, 1998), 15.

6. L. Newbery, *Catcall*, 28.

the audience's attention is guided to assimilate and understand the text alongside the image in such a persuasive way to achieve the intended informative result. Twentieth century appears to be a time of expansion of various genres with multimedia character whose nature and impact of their message rely on the integration of words and images.[7]

Finally, the translator's decision needs to be well informed in relation to the achievements of the relevant scholarship. Newmark's conclusion in this regard will bring a valuable input to the present discussion. He maintains that preservation of Latinisms in English is advisable due to the benefits of their characteristics to the TT versus their translated version. The short form of Latin words in contrast to their translations will preserve the text's clarity, precision and unity. The formal character of Latinisms will benefit more to the official text's register.[8]

4.2. Toward Constructing the Most Suitable Device to Preserve and Transmit the Facts and Data Element into Romanian

Desmidt warns that sometimes close adherence to the literary elements of the ST suffers from adopted pedagogical intentions by the translator and business considerations by the publisher. When the translators in view of the level of comprehension of their young readers strive to adapt the

---

7. Gregor Goethals, "Images of Translation," in *(Multi) Media Translation: Concepts, Practices, and Research*. Translation Library, vol.35, eds. Yves Gambier and Henrik Gottlieb Benjamins (Amsterdam/Philadelphia: John Benjamins Publishing Company, 2001), 46.

8. The following example has been provided: "... a fortiori is stronger than 'all the more so' and shorter than 'for similar and more convincing reasons.'" Peter Newmark, *Paragraphs on Translation*. Topics in Translation 1 (Clevedon, UK: Multilingual Matters Ltd, 1993), 8.

Constructing Suitable Facts and Data Device for Romanian

content, structures and style of the ST they estrange the literary quality of the ST from the TT. Furthermore this gap is maintained by the publisher when due to financial limitations the visual aids of the text in picture books are diminished.[9] This critique underlines further the importance of the translator's decision and the presence of visual aids for the reader.

One of the most extraordinary features of picture books is the use of metafictive devices through which the plot of the book overcomes literary limitations and communicates a message of the interwoven text and picture providing close interaction of the readers with the text.[10] The above mentioned device contains such a level of intertextuality. The page itself, containing the Latin terms and the handwriting style of Josh is part of *Josh's Book of Cats* and by the presence of these features encourages the reader to a new level of interaction. The nature of the picture books is formalised through interrelation between picture and text which creates a tension in communicating their message to the children readership. This inherited tension in the nature of the picture books brings them to the position of being a challenge to their readership to the extent that the comprehension of their content may go beyond the readers' interpretative abilities. The examination of this nature through the means of postmodernist theory leads to revealing the integration of its opposing characteristics of

---

9. Isabelle Desmidt, "A Prototypical Approach within Descriptive Translation Studies? Colliding Norms in Translated Children's Literature," in *Children's Literature in Translation: Challenges and Strategies*, eds. Jan Van Coillie & Walter P. Verschueren (Manchester, UK: St. Jerome Publishing, 2006), 88.

10. David Lewis, "The Constructedness of Texts: Picture Books and the Metafictive," in *Only Connect: Readings on Children's Literature*, 3rd ed., eds. Sheila Egoff, Gordon Stubbs, Ralph Ashley, and Wendy Sutton (Oxford: Oxford University Press, 1996), 274, 275.

simplicity versus complexity as well as encouraging versus troubling impact on their readers.[11]

In my attempt to preserve the humoristic effect in the previously mentioned extract, it is of crucial importance to deal appropriately with the Latin terms. Hence I will make every effort to focus on the presence of the Latin terminology and its similarities in relations to the Latin names presented in the text. The focus of my device for transmitting the English vernacular in the aforementioned extract will be constructed on Josh's statement: "I am not making that up" which I have translated as "Nu inventez eu asta." The verb "a inventa" in Romanian carries both the meaning of "making something up" and also "to invent or to create."[12] Therefore, the humoristic effect would be perceived from the perspective of the existent similarities with Latin. Hence Josh's statement is valid that he does not create the similarities between the Romanian and Latin register in the specific case of Latin names but they are there in the text. This similarity brings to the attention of the reader that indeed there is something funny about the fact that the animal names in Latin and Romanian sound alike or have something in common. Thus, they are going to be presented successively for in order to reflect their similarities not their contrast as is the case in English. Reconstructing the scientific device for the TL by changing the focus of humoristic effect, the intended effect to produce surprise is still maintained in the TL but the translator has personalised it to match the

11. Geoff Moss, "Metafiction, Illustration, and the Poetics of Children's Literature," in *Literature for Children: Contemporary Criticism*, ed. Peter Hunt (London: Routledge, 1992; reprint, 2003), 51, 52, 66.

12. *A inventa* [To invent]. Industrial Soft, 2009, [online], Available at http://dictionare.com/phpdic/roen40.php?field0=a+inventa, Accessed on 16 July 2009.

Constructing Suitable Facts and Data Device for Romanian

expected effect on the readership in line with the character of the TL and the language norms.

It is important to underline the fact that the process of transformation of the ST into TT would undergo change of the language forms with the purpose to retain the message of the ST.[13] The degree of transformation is related to the languages, dissimilarity and the divergence between their cultural aspects. The more parallels are defined between the languages the less form alteration needs to take place.[14]

To better illustrate the contrastive approach in building the humoristic effect in the scientific text, I will represent the construction of the intended effect both in the ST and then in the TL as reconstructed by the translator.

The humoristic effect in the ST as built by the author on the contrastive elements based on format and sounds between the Latin and English terminology:

Latin names	No obvious relationship	English names
Felidae	≠	Cat family
Turdus viscivorus	≠	Mistle trush
Turdus philomelos	≠	Song Trush
Turdus	≠	Thrush family

Josh's central statement: "I am not making that up"—the contrast is obvious. Therefore, "I am not making that

---

13. Landers also maintains that the principal concern is to keep the tone in the recreated word play. Clifford E. Landers, *Literary Translation: A Practical Guide.* Topics in Translation, ed. Geoffrey Samuelsson-Brown, vol. 22 (Clevedon, UK: Multilingual Matters Ltd, 2001), 109.

14. Eugene A. Nida and Charles R. Taber, *The Theory and Practice of Translation.* Helps for Translators Prepared under the Auspices of the United Bible Societies, vol.VIII (Leiden, The Netherlands: E. J. Brill, 1969; second reprint, 1982), 5.

up" leads to the humoristic effect and the element of surprise due to the contrasting terminology.

The humoristic effect in the TL as built by the translator on the similarities between elements based on format and sounds between the Latin and Romanian terminology:

Effect obtained by similarities in the two languages

Felidae = Feline

Turdus viscivorus = sturzul de vâsc

Turdus philomelos = sturzul cântător

Turdus = sturzul

Josh's central statement: "I am not making that up"—recreated in the TL and translated as: "Nu inventez eu asta"—the similarities are obvious.

Therefore, "I am not making that up" *Nu inventez eu asta* leads to the humoristic effect and the element of surprise due to the similar terminology between the two languages and finally pointed out by Josh.

4.3. Presentation of the Embodiment of the Facts and Data Element of English Vernacular through the Distinctiveness of Romanian Language of Young Adults

Such a format as the one revealed in the data and facts element which incorporates Latin and presents particularities of Josh's handwriting style and images of lions either drawn or cut up from magazines and then glued in his *Book of Cats* can be defined as a sort of metafiction that Newbery decided to weave within the story for a greater effect on the readership. Dealing with metafiction in children literature, Moss had identified its presence in two forms. On the one hand,

Constructing Suitable Facts and Data Device for Romanian

the author shares his character through revelatory perspective of the world by means of a text which provides transparency avoiding exposure of constructive methods and relying on the readers' openness. On the other hand, similar author's intentions are identified in a text which lacks transparency, exposes its methodological means and blurs the relationship between fiction and reality. The discontinuity between these two is identified in the clarity of the message dependant on the obscuring role of the textual methodological format.[15] The metafictional dimension of the present text underlines the difficulty of bridging the ST and the TT and requires special attention during the process of translation.

Having already explained in the previous section the choice of building the humoristic effect around Josh's statement "I am not making that up," the translation of the extract is presented and integrated in the TL as follows:

> Familia felinelor este *felidae*. Toate organismele din univers au un nume latin, deci nu contează de la ce limbă pornești, numele științific e întodeauna la fel. Deci ființele umane sunt *homo sapiens*. Uneori numele sunt ușor de ținut minte, ca și bondarul care e *bombus bombus* și pitulicea e *troglodytes troglodytes*. Nume mare pentru o pasăre foarte mică. Și familia sturzilor se numește *turdus*. Nu inventez eu asta. *Turdus viscivorus* e sturzul de vâsc și *turdus philomelos* e sturzul cântător. Din nou la feline, pisica domestică e *felis catus*, de aceea multe pisici sunt numite Felix, de asemenea Felix e o mâncare pentru pisici.

One can notice that there are also some apparent dissimilarities in format between some of the Latin names and Romanian ones like in "pitulicea" *troglodytes troglodytes*

---

15. G. Moss, *Metafiction, Illustration, and the Poetics of Children's Literature*, 45.

and "pisica domestică" *felis catus*. However, this apparent discontinuity in the format does not conflict with the intended meaning in the original. "Pitulicea" is defined as "a small bird" in *DEX*[16] which is in line with the following sentence: *Nume mare pentru o pasăre foarte mică* "Big name for a very small bird."

---

16. "Pitulicea" [Wren], *DEX online: Dicționare explicative ale limbii române* [DEX online: Explanatory Dictionaries of the Romanian Language], [online], Available at http://www.dictionare.com/phpdic/dex.php?field0=pitulice, Accessed on 16 July 2009.

5

Constructing Suitable Word Play Device for Romanian

5.1. *Evaluating and Establishing the English Word Play Device as the Specific Element of the English Vernacular*

DEALING WITH DOMESTICATION AND foreignisation when translating children's literature raises the scholarly debate of the use of either of these methods to a new level. The positive side of the foreignisation with its exposure of the young readers to the uncommon and unusual foreign elements of the text appears to be profitable for their development but inconsiderate of the diverse readership. The domestication may be considered as being part of every translation as the interpretive presence of the embedded child image in the translator's point of view. The dilemma of impartiality rises beyond the use of these two approaches reaching to the world view of the translator, i.e. ideology, ethics, childhood understanding being inevitable part of the method employed.[1]

---

1. Riitta Oittinen, "No Innocent Act: On the Ethics of Translating

Monica Augustina Zhekov

There are mutual grounds between the original writing and translation when the process of transformation is envisioned in the act of moulding the original to produce a new expression of its essence when change of genre is in view as in the original writing or change of language, as in translation. However, these two operate within a restrictive framework which is specially demanding for the translation due to the necessity for transmitting the original meaning of the ST.[2] The constraints are much greater for the translation than for the original writing. The translator needs to show awareness and deal with the entire body of constraints regarding the context, genre and language of the original, the continuity between the viewpoint of the author and his own and various cultural and linguistic discontinuities between the source and target texts. Textual coherence should also be a fundamental characteristic of a translation and in particular of wordplay. Hence the translator's task is to achieve this logical structure of the TT either through reorganising the compositional pattern of the ST or creating a new structural format of the TT using its linguistic resources.[3] The overwhelming burden of constraints, however, can produce a strong impulse for creativity for the translator, challenging him to discover successful approaches to deal with the restrictive framework and ultimately empower new dimensions of his creativeness.[4]

for Children," in *Children's Literature in Translation: Challenges and Strategies*, eds. Jan Van Coillie & Walter P. Verschueren (Manchester, UK: St. Jerome Publishing, 2006), 43.

2. Jean Boase-Beier and Michael Holman, eds., *The Practices of Literary Translation: Constraints and Creativity* (Manchester, UK: St. Jerome Publishing, 1999), 4.

3. Albrecht Neubert and Gregory M. Shreve, *Translation as Text*. Translation Studies, eds. Albrecht Neubert, Gert Jager and Gregory M. Shreve (Kent, Ohio: The Kent State University Press, 1992), 102.

4. Jean Boase-Beier and Michael Holman, eds., *The Practices of Literary Translation: Constraints and* Creativity, 13.

Constructing Suitable Word Play Device for Romanian

A great deal of creativity is demanded from the translator in dealing with the word play device which is constructed around cultural indicators as e.g. *West Ham football team* and other items of the characters' familiar context. The translator will attempt to keep the cultural element where possible but she would most likely have to recreate the word play in the TL because of the lack of compatibility regarding the suitable vocabulary which can maintain the characteristics of the word play, namely words starting with *O* which can be categorised as allusive words or cues for unlocking the game meaning. Deeply rooted into the cultural milieu of the text, the literary form of allusions creates significant difficulty to the translator due to its familiarity to the native readers of the domestic text but not to the readers of the foreign text. The translators need to accept their limitations in transforming this literary device in its exactness.[5]

The difficulty of translating allusive wordplay being more culturally related than linguistically associated may be at least partly overcome through understanding of the diverse cultural awareness of relatively homogeneous readers' group. Hence the choice of the particular method of translation of allusive wordplay to be implemented should rely on translator's knowledge of the potential readers.[6]

---

5. Ritva Leppihalme, "Caught in the Frame: A Target-Culture Viewpoint on Allusive Wordplay," *The Translator* 2/2 (November 1996): 215.

6. Ibid., 216.

Monica Augustina Zhekov

5.2. Toward Constructing the Most Suitable Word Play Device to Preserve and Transmit the Word Play Element into Romanian

Leppihalme argues that when the wordplay is in view in the process of translation the choice of appropriate approach should be consequent to the localisation of the identical linguistic form in the ST.[7] The very nature of a wordplay, occurrences of diverse meaning form word/s related by form or sound in an arbitrary linguistic framework, poses serious problems to the translator who may need to mould the wordplay in the TT in order to achieve the intended meaning by words neither similar in form nor sound.[8] That is the present case when the translator has to find solutions in order to match the overall requirement of the wordplay: to provide words starting with *O* which are part of the group of words familiar to the target reader and are relevant to the game but in the same time able to transmit the vernacular element in its best shape. In order to do that, the translator needs to introduce to the Romanian readership the challenging marks of the English cultural context such as e.g. *West Ham football team* which is representative for the original readership. In addition to that, in order to maintain the vernacular element the translator will preserve these marks.

Another element to consider which contributes to the present discussion is that of secrecy. The nature of secrecy in children's literature reveals a two-dimensional character. On the one hand, it shows the effort of the author to

---

7. R. Leppihalme, *Caught in the Frame: A Target-Culture Viewpoint on Allusive Wordplay*, 199.

8. Rachel Weissbrod, "'Curiouser and Curiouser:' Hebrew Translations of Wordplay in Alice Adventures in Wonderland," *The Translator* 2/2 (November 1996): 223.

Constructing Suitable Word Play Device for Romanian

understand the child imagination, its capacity and limits coming from the stand point characterised with the dynamics of adult life. On the other hand, it presents the young reader dealing with the secrets from within their unique perspective and forming their ways as a person for their own development and as a part of the society.[9]

Once again the complexity of the picture books substantiated in the relationship between pictures and text needs to be underlined since its dynamics impact the present discussion. The unique nature of the picture books is characterised by the diverse ways through which their message is communicated to the readers. The same message being conveyed through two different vehicles, pictures and words, creates tension in the nature of the message and in the way it is represented by its two mediums. The later tension is formalised in the diversity of the representation of the message by pictures and words. The message is enriched by its two sources but the validity of their content is challenged by the difference in the representations. The tension in the nature of the message is sustained by the insight of the readers and their ability to understand the restrictive and deformed character of the worldview that is being expressed.[10] To add to the complexity of the present word game, Newbery includes personal touches of Jamie such as drawing of what can be either *o* (zero) or *O* (the letter O) in Jamie's handwriting. Oitttinen also underlines that an important element of the relationship between illustrations and text is the cursive writing. It provides further more vibrant dynamic of this relationship.

---

9. John Daniel Stahl, "The Imaginative Uses of Secrecy in Children's Literature," in *Only Connect: Readings on Children's Literature*, 3rd ed., eds. Sheila Egoff, Gordon Stubbs, Ralph Ashley and Wendy Sutton (Oxford: Oxford University Press, 1996), 39.

10. Perry Nodelman, "Decoding the Images: Illustration and Picture Books," in *Understanding Children's Literature*, ed. Peter Hunt (London: Routledge, 1999), 79.

Monica Augustina Zhekov

This significant feature of the ST needs to be taken in consideration and its influence on the TT decided according to the comfortability of the target audience with it.[11]

To deal with the lexical inconsistencies between English and Romanian, I will attempt to select Romanian correspondents from a familiar category, suitable to the targeted readership. Looking at the original design of the game in the ST, we can notice that Newbery did not group the words starting with O or o in any hyponymy relationship which may have reflected a different relationship into the TL.[12] Her concern seems to be only to select the words that her target readership, between 11 and 16 years old could comprehend and be familiar with. Thus, she selects her vocabulary from the categories such as: elements of nature (oxygen), varieties of fruit (orange) and animals, including sea animals and birds, (Orang-utan, Okapi, Ostrich, Octopus, Owl, and Osprey). In the process of transformation wherever possible and applicable the translator had used the correspondent term in the TL, e.g. *oxigen* "oxygen" but avoided to translate "okapi" as *okapi* because of the lack of evidence in the TL that this animal is known well enough to the target readership. Therefore, the translator has chosen to use a general term *oraș* "city" which meets both criteria set by the author in the ST, that of familiarity to the reader and to start with O. Concerning the rest of the component words in the game, namely, orange, owl, octopus, ostrich, orang-utan and osprey, their Romanian correspondents do not start with the letter O as illustrated on the next page:

11. R. Oittinen, *Translating for Children*, 102.

12. Malmkjaer illustrates such possible variations giving the example of the difference in category for "potato" in English and French. Kirsten Malmkjaer, *Linguistics and the Language of Translation* (Edinburg: Edinburg University Press, 2005; reprint, 2007), 105.

Constructing Suitable Word Play Device for Romanian

Lack of compatibility in the words starting with O in the ST which do not meet the criterion in TL:

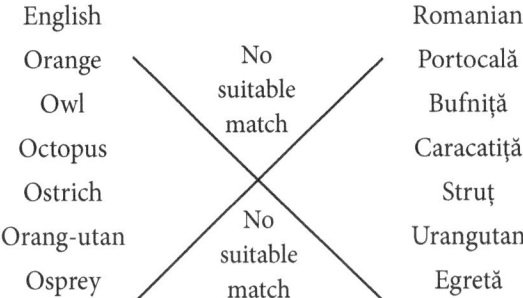

English		Romanian
Orange		Portocală
Owl	No suitable match	Bufniță
Octopus		Caracatiță
Ostrich		Struț
Orang-utan	No suitable match	Urangutan
Osprey		Egretă

List of choices that the translator makes in order to match the criteria of familiarity for the TL reader and to start with O:

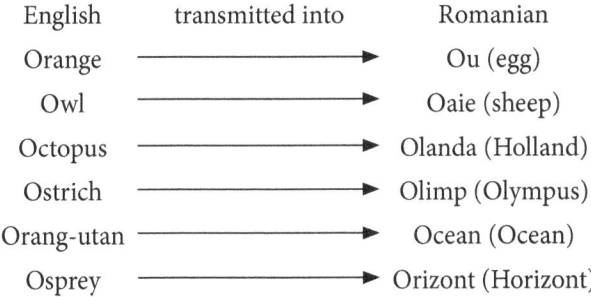

English	transmitted into	Romanian
Orange	→	Ou (egg)
Owl	→	Oaie (sheep)
Octopus	→	Olanda (Holland)
Ostrich	→	Olimp (Olympus)
Orang-utan	→	Ocean (Ocean)
Osprey	→	Orizont (Horizon)

From the above choices, one can notice that the translator has chosen words which are easily understood by a young reader (between the age of 11 and 16), and which do not pose any difficulty for this group of readers. Therefore they meet the criteria of familiarity and also start with *O*.

Monica Augustina Zhekov

5.3. Presentation of the Embodiment of the Word Play Element of English Vernacular through the Distinctiveness of Romanian Language of Young Adults

Tackling wordplay is one of the most difficult tasks of the translator from which stands out dealing with puns. The wordplay communicates the intention of the writer to bring to light uniqueness of a character and can be expressed using various forms such as "puns, alliterations, coinages, malapropisms, hypercorrections, and the whole range of verbal resources."[13] Due to the specific habits of the readers, translating children's literature requires much more flexibility with the text than translating for adults. Landers suggests that it may be due to this demanding character of the audience that a quite close similarity has been established between the principles for writing children's literature and those for its translation.[14]

The complexity of wordplay should be acknowledged in the fact that it may be part of variety of texts, in single or multiple occurrences, in all literary dimensions of the text, e.g. syntax or structure, and not with only humoristic effect. The interpretation of wordplay is also loaded with complexity being related to "the sound/meaning associations of language(s)."[15] My translation underneath imple-

13. The way forward with translating puns is accepting the impossibility of literary translation and strive to achieve the puns' effect through changing its setting in order to preserve the double meaning and its tone. C. E. Landers, *Literary Translation: A Practical Guide*, 109, 110.

14. Ibid., 108.

15. Salvatore Attardo, "Translation and Humour: An Approach Based on the General Theory of Verbal Humour (GTVH)," *The Translator: Studies in Intercultural Communication* 8/2 (November 2002): 189.

Constructing Suitable Word Play Device for Romanian

ments the criteria discussed in the previous section, that of familiarity and the *O* words and where possible implements words from the same field, e.g. locations: Ol*anda*—Holland and Ol*imp*—Olympus, are both locations and the first two letters of each word are identical (ol) for a better corresponding sound. The same principle, of the parallel sounds is applied to O*rizont*—Horizon and O*raș*—city. In the case of Orang-utan here replaced by O*ceeean* (Ocean)—Ocean, the translator has integrated additional vowels (two additional letters *e*) into the actual form of the Romanian *ocean* whose spelling is exactly like in the English "ocean." That choice was based on the length of the sound for "Orangutan" for which the translator found "Oceeean" as the most suitable option. The latter being constrained by the previously mentioned limits of words starting with O from a familiar register to the young reader and here also trying to imitate the length of the word "Orang-utan" and the slight similarity in the pronunciation; both words finish in "an." Underneath the reader can see how the choices made by the translator and discussed earlier are now incorporated in the translation of the extract.

> Jamie luase creionul și i-a atins vârfu cu degetul. Îl luase cu amândouă mâinile și-l răsucea între degetul mare și cel arătător. Îl priveam gândindu-mă: glumește cu noi făcându-ne să așteptăm. În cele din urmă, a apucat creionul cu mâna dreaptă, s-a aplecat peste foaie și desenă, cu mare grijă, un *o*.
>
> Mama se aplecă dornică înainte, așteptând mai multe, dar asta a fost tot. Un *o*.
>
> "O! Ce înseamnă asta, un O? O sau nimic?"
>
> Jamie a pus creionul jos și s-a lăsat pe spătarul scaunului. Mama și cu mine ne uitam lung la el, dar el nu se uita la niciunul dintre

noi—se uita spre fereastră cu acea privirea goală și ciudată cu care mă obișnuisem.

"Ce înseamnă asta, Jamie? începui să ghicesc. Zero? Zero—ca și scorul lui West Ham de sâmbăta trecută? Un cerc? Un inel? Un cerc pentru gimnastică? O de la ou? Oxigen? Sau de la oaie . . . Olanda . . . Olimp?"

Jamie se uita la mine și puteam vedea că-l interesa jocul ăsta.

"Oceeean? încercai eu. Orizont? Oraș?"

Luase creionul și desenase cu grijă în interiorul acelui O.

6

Constructing Suitable Web Page Device For Romanian

6.1. Evaluating and Establishing the English Web Page Device as the Specific Element of the English Vernacular

THE VERNACULAR WEB PAGE element is defined by the navigation, buttons and the layout of the page. The text itself does not carry a particularity of the English vernacular as its content is based on a foreign myth about the Korat cat. The translation of the ST elements, namely, the navigation, buttons and layout would nevertheless aim to transmit into Romanian the representative English vernacular.

Information technology and the internet, which continuously extend their influence on young people, slowly find their place in the literature targeting this group of readers.[1]

---

1. According to Applebaum, electronic elements such as web pages and Internet jargon are currently used more and more in the contemporary literature for children. Noga Applebaum, "Electronic Texts and Adolescent Agency: Computers and the Internet in Contemporary Children's Fiction," in *Modern Children's Literature: An Introduction*, ed. Kimberley Reynolds (New York: Palgrave Macmillan, 2005), 252.

Monica Augustina Zhekov

The main struggle with implementing more technologically defined elements in a story appears to be the tension between the author's and readers' IT knowledge. Young readers seem to advance much faster in understanding and dealing with IT than the adult writers. However, in spite of this tension, the content of children and young adults' literature are increasingly enriched with IT defined elements due to their well acknowledged literary potential.[2]

Newbery also appeals to the young readership with such items integrating IT and internet web pages in the actual text. The integration of such elements may be defined as a metafictional representation. Thus, it is important to have a closer look at the use of this specific element in children's literature. The methods of narrative presentation employed in metafiction and experimental fiction of children's writings include various disruptive developments, use of intertextuality, parody and of various narrative forms, integrating narrative unit identical to the main narrative, use of multiple narrator's view points and shift in relationships, employing narrator's voice intrusion and incorporation of historical language to deal with fiction and reality. These tend to widen the gap between the reader and the text. The reader's conventionally developed mindset of anticipated narrative development and conclusion is further challenged. More interpretive power is envisioned for the implied readers. Employing narrative techniques should lead the readers of metafiction to associate the obtained message with the events from everyday life.[3]

Even though some may consider that this kind of disruption in a novel such as *Catcall* may minimise the

2. Ibid., 251.

3. Robyn McCallum, "Very Advanced Texts: Metafictions and Experimental Work," in *Understanding Children's Literature*, ed. Peter Hunt (London: Routledge, 1999), 139, 142–49.

overall quality of the work and the smooth development of the story line, I would agree with Oittinen that the quality of the TT of illustrated children's literature depends on the holistic transformation of the message of the ST including its visual elements. The latter does not relate only to illustrations but also to the complete text layout including its format and headings' style. Hence the translator needs to deal with both the author's and illustrator's points of view in order to achieve a fare treatment of the ST transforming it into the TT.[4]

6.2. Toward Constructing the Most Suitable Web Page Device to Preserve and Transmit the English Web Page Element into Romanian

The visual characteristics of the ST in children's picture books play a significant contributory part to its message. Hence their transformation into the TT is essential and beneficial for any target audience.[5] Much consideration should be given to the layout of the metafictional elements in picture books since their translation undergoes a unique dimension related to their specific nature. This is the transformation of the relationship between pictures and text. Hence the translator is not only engaged with communicating the message of the text through the TL to the target readers but also is concerned to relate the interconnection between images and words. This relationship should not be communicated through words but through lack of words, i.e. spatial occurrences, which may preserve the interplay

---

4. R. Oittinen, *Translating for Children*, 102.
5. R. Oittinen, *Translating for Children*, 103.

and place the target audience in the same interpretive position as the original readers.[6]

The complexity of the present device necessitates consideration of another issue, namely the relationship between internet technologies and subject unveiling information through word indicators. The internet communication between individuals and organisation revolutionised the accessibility of resources and their interconnectivity. Through the means of the "World Wide Web" and the "hyper text markup language (html)" topical interrelations within a subject area have become foundational for the subject's complete unveiling. The new technologically advanced communication has placed a demand for presentation of clear word indicators on the Web Pages which would bring a cohesive and comprehensive treatment of the particular subject. Hence dealing with narrative would require hypertext consisting of substantial word indicators such as "identity, representation, time, space, signs and technologies"[7] to give a fair scope of the subject matter in view and to facilitate the topical interrelations to further specific information related to each of these words.[8]

Before making a decision on how the web page vernacular element will be transmitted into the TL, the translator will have to analyse the expectations of the Romanian readership taking into account the design and the content of other web pages that are browsed by those who love animals. However in order to maintain the English vernacular

---

6. Emer O'Sullivan, "Translating Pictures," in *The Translation of Children's Literature: A Reader*, ed. Gillian Lathey, *Topics in Translation* 31, eds. Susan Bassnett and Edwm Gentzler (Clevedon, UK: Multilingual Matters Ltd, 2006), 113.

7. Paul Cobley, *Narrative: The New Critical Idiom* (London: Routledge, 2001; reprint, 2003), 203.

8. Ibid.

in the newly constructed web page, the translator may have to make a decision in regard to which are those English specific elements to be transferred in the TL and which ones should be customised to suit the target readership's Internet behaviour. There are three significant elements to consider before developing a website, namely, the targeted audience, the nature of the site and the renewal of its content. Thinking about the potential visitors to be reached, consideration should be given to factors such as their age, position in society, educational background and web surfing skills. When the nature of the website is in question, two main variants to consider are informational or entertaining. In this regard the nature of the website should suit the characteristics of the targeted audience. An important role to the creation of the site will play the structure and its content that will be arranged in various topical levels. The eventual renewal of the completed website is important in regard to the necessity of the content update, its frequency, the source of the update and the person responsible for the update.[9]

After finalising the plan for the main characteristics of the website function, constructive decisions should be made in regard to its web pages. The web pages should be considered in their entirety as elements of the whole site and part of its established functionality. Hence alienated design of a web page should be avoided specially in light of the potential changes coming from the subsequent development of the other pages and the links established with them. The holistic planning of the web pages should be undertaken with care and precision which may be benefited by manual drawing of a map of the web pages within

---

9. Timothy D. Green, Abbie Brown, LeAnne Robinson, *Making the Most of the Web in Your Classroom: A Teacher's Guide to Blogs, Podcasts, Wikis, Pages, and Sites* (Thousand Oaks: Corwin Press, 2008), 91.

the framework of the whole site.[10] The multiplicity of web pages in a website requires establishment of their connections which constitutes a navigation chart. The significance of these relations between the web pages within a website should be reflected in a preparatory process of designing the navigation chart. The preservation of the holistic structure of the chart requires a visualised approach to the planning in which all the pages are visible and their relations may be clearly established. This can be achieved through turning the web pages into Post it Notes placed on a sheet of paper where in a clear and visually presentable way the links between different pages are drawn.[11]

The final stage of producing a website involves building the individual web pages and using the previously established plan integrating them into the whole and adding any additional media elements. This process will require further work of creation, incorporation and adjustment of various prepared and new website segments which may involve also graphics, sound and video files. This stage may also involve developing, editing and transferring the texts from the commonly used word-processing software to the web pages.[12]

Another dimension of the approach to the present device refers to the critical tools used by the translator. Assessment of multimedia translation, part of which is website translation, should not follow the same standards as the one produced from conventional text due to its diverse communicative forms which prioritise its characteristics of "comprehensibility, accessibility and usability."[13] The importance of

10. Ibid., 92.

11. Ibid., 93.

12. Ibid., 94.

13. Yves Gambier and Henrik Gottlieb, eds., *(Multi) Media Translation: Concepts, Practices, and Research*. Benjamins Translation Library, eds. Yves Gambier and Henrik Gottlieb, vol. 34 (Amsterdam/Philadelphia: John Benjamins Publishing Company, 2001), xi.

the functionality of the source and its appeal to its audience lead to valuation which cannot simply rely on the standard linguistic format and identification of mistakes in the text.[14]

Another aspect of this device which contributes to its use in the process of translation is its impact on the readers and their imagination. The technologically advanced sources of presentation of narrative, TV and computer, provide extended means for looking at its various aspects, details, characters, elements which underline a new dimension of dealing with the story, "the power of the reader."[15] The author's aim with using imageries in children's books is not only to offer an alternative depiction of reality but also to impact readers' imagination. Hence through specific emphasis on details and use of language which accommodates such articulation, the writer triggers reader's imagination toward illumination or excitement from the text.[16]

The approach of the user to the website surfed goes beyond the straightforward logical order of dealing with a text. The user may move through the webpage in various and diverse ways linking different parts of the texts at different times which may not be subdued to any formal pattern or logic. This approach to the multimedia source inevitably impacts its translation.[17] As there is no straightforward standard of how the Romanian websites are designed and which are their distinct characteristics in comparison to the English ones, the translator has to make her own decision on the most suitable format to transfer the English vernacular element represented by the website incorporated in the novel. However, the common element shared by the Romanian

14. Ibid., xi, xii.
15. P. Cobley, *Narrative: The New Critical Idiom*, 205.
16. R. J. Lukens, *A Critical Handbook of Children's Literature*, 198.
17. Y. Gambier and H. Gottlieb, eds., *(Multi) Media Translation: Concepts, Practices, and Research*, xviii.

websites which are tailored for those interested in wild animals and their habitat are the graphic effects which most of the time constitute the focus of the home page.[18] The distinct element of the Romanian web pages is the option to select the language in which the reader chooses to read/browse the page. Most of the time one can make the choice of language between English and Romanian but also some websites provide the option to choose between English, Romanian and Hungarian. However, other languages can be accessible according to the targeted group of visitors. Because of the speed by which the web page development progresses, one can notice that even though *Catcall* is a rather new book, first published in 2006, the incorporated web page design is rather outdated. The simple design format of the web page can lead the translator to the conclusion that the particular design is specific to the format of the web pages built about three years ago to which constraints of the designer's abilities apply, primarily due to the available web design tools in 2006.[19] In the current web pages of Cotswold Wildlife Park[20] and ZSL London Zoo,[21] the updated design is much more

---

18. The same trend is noticed in the following web pages, part of the websites of Oradea Zoo, Timişoara Zoo and Târgu-Mureş Zoo. *Oradea Zoo*, [online], Available at http://www.zooradea.ro/index.php?s=&id_fm=&lang=en, Accessed on 14 July 2009; *Timişoara Zoo*, [online], Available at http://www.zootimisoara.ro/, Accessed on 14 July 2009; *Târgu-Mureş Zoo*, [online], Available at http://www.zootirgumures.ro/, Accessed on 14 July 2009.

19. Nowadays very few websites provide their visitors with the date when the websites were built. No such information is provided on the website of *ZSL London Zoo* or *Cotswold Wildlife Park* which was visited by Josh and Jamie. *ZSL London Zoo*, [online], Available at http://www.zsl.org/, Accessed on 15 July 2009; *Cotswold Wildlife Park*, [online], Available at http://www.cotswoldwildlifepark.co.uk/index.php, Accessed on 15 July 2009.

20. *Cotswold Wildlife Park*, [online].

21. *ZSL London Zoo*, [online].

complex than the one presented in the *Catcall*. Nevertheless, the webpage of Cotswold Wildlife Park still presents a simple navigation arranged in the left-hand side of the page with some quick links in the right hand side of the page. Concerning the navigation and the links, the web page of ZSL London Zoo presents a more similar pattern to the one presented by Newbery, namely, having left-hand navigation and horizontal menu at the top of the web page. Therefore, based on the similarities of design and navigation, the translator maintains that the best representation of the web page English vernacular in the set extract is a modified web page. This modification takes into account the present developments of the web page design in both ZSL London Zoo (UK) and Târgu-Mureş Zoo (Romania) and transmits the texts and character of the web page implemented by Newbery in *Catcall*. Thus, the proposed web page being vehicle of the English vernacular reflecting a web page existent only in the English context would maintain the English wording of the buttons and navigation having its content text translated into Romanian. With the understanding that the Romanian readership has basic knowledge of English, the presence of the English buttons would not appear to be restrictive to the reading behaviour but would be revelatory in regard to the original context of the web page. Other design features such as images and colours can be also maintained in line with other English websites in the field.

When making the decision of what kind of web page the translator should represent, she needs to take into account the behaviour and abilities of the researcher who visits the web page for finding the required information. The researcher accessing the web for collecting data needs to posses the knowledge of its search vehicles and the ability to use them. Two main means are providing the searching facility of the web, namely, indexes and search engines. Indexes' approach to collecting data is the systematic collection and arrangement of information contained in the web sites under trees of categories. In this way the information needed is located through narrowing the subject matter of the research to particular topic. One of the world's well known web indexes is Yahoo. Search engines function through a software programme which gathers the information from the websites through keywords and "Boolean terms (and, or, and not are Boolean terms)."[22] Once gathered, the information is arranged in a database which is accessible and explorable through the means of the search interface. One of the world's most used search engines is Google.[23]

The researchers are to continuously improve their behaviour and abilities for obtaining the necessary information. Thus, the researchers are encouraged to develop such abilities by creating their own website project. The main purpose of engaging students to deal with the web as part of their classroom activities should be to obtain the knowledge from the information acquired and to become acquainted with its standards. The important elements of the web assignments may be regarded as its accomplished final form, the process of developing it and most of all its content. Knowledge and appropriate use of the technological means for achieving the results are important but they should not overshadow the main characteristics of the assignment.[24]

---

22. T. D. Green, A. Brown, L. Robinson, *Making the Most of the Web in Your Classroom: A Teacher's Guide to Blogs, Podcasts, Wikis, Pages, and Sites*, 35.

23. Ibid.

24. Ibid., 60.

6.3. Presentation of the Embodiment of the Web Page Element of English Vernacular through the Distinctiveness of Romanian Language of Young Adults

The significance of metafictional texts in children's literature such as web page extracts should be underlined due to their impact on the readers and their role in relation to other texts. Children readership is interested in metafictional texts since they provide continuous source of attraction through their diverse and unpredictable nature. Metafictional texts go beyond the ordinary texts, challenging their limitations, exceeding their abilities and reforming them through developing the genre as a whole.[25] The notion that metafictional texts are too difficult for children is unsustainable in light of the children's ability to tackle various literary devices as part of a plot which is developing in a culturally familiar context.[26]

Following the strategy presented in the previous section, the translator has successfully transferred the vernacular element incorporated in the web page device from the ST into Romanian. By maintaining the buttons and the links' text in English but having the main text translated into Romanian, the translator had introduced to the target readership the foreign cultural element which sends a signal to the reader that the web page in front of them is a translation. This is an equivalent strategy to the one *Google Translator*[27] operates on

---

[25]. G. Moss, *Metafiction, Illustration, and the Poetics of Children's Literature*, 51.

[26]. C. Sarland, "The Secret Seven vs. the Twits: Cultural Clash or Cosy Combination?" *Signal* 42 (1983): 107, quoted in G. Moss, *Metafiction, Illustration, and the Poetics of Children's Literature*, 46.

[27]. *Google Translate*, [online], Available at http://translate.google.com/#, Accessed on 20 July 2009.

when translating foreign web pages into English. In this case, *Google Translator,* which is a machine translator, translates the foreign text contained in the home page into English but the buttons are left in the original language. That is because most of the time the buttons and the links of the websites are either images (usually having an extension such as .jpg, .gif or .jpeg) or other multimedia such as flash with a .swf extension (Shock Wave Flash), which cannot be recognised as text by a machine translator. Due to the familiarity of most Internet users with the *Google Translator's* strategy, I consider that a similar strategy as the one employed in constructing the present device in the TL would be the easiest to comprehend by the target readership and a suitable translation tool to incorporate the strange/foreign cultural element into the Romanian language.

From the presentation of the web page element in the TL below, one may notice that the translator had followed the left and top of the page menu pattern of the original web page presented by Newbery. However, the current web page presents the quick links opposite to the banner (at the bottom of the page); a decision established with the view to help the reader access faster the main pages of the website without having to go back to the top of the page to obtain access. Due to the text type limitation concerning the use of Romanian diacritics and their visibility in the Internet Explorer, the translator had made differentiation between the fonts using the white colour font for the quoted text and for the subject of the action (Rain Cloud Cat) described between the quotation marks. The reader is supplied underneath with the translation of the extract that is incorporated into the web page device since the small font size in the web page image may obstruct the reading.

> Acest mit provine din Siam, care e acum Tailanda. Ei au o pisică numită Korat, de culoare

Constructing Suitable Web Page Device For Romanian

albastru-gri. Culoarea gri a acesteia e ca a norului de ploaie și fermierii luau pisica la o procesiune când aveau nevoie de ploaie pentru recoltele lor. Fermierii se roagă la zeii cerului și se stropește apă pe fața pisicii, care se crede să aducă ploaie.

Un poet din Tailanda a compus o poezie despre pisica nor-de-ploaie:

> "Perii sunt netezi
> Cu rădăcini ca norii,
> Și vârfuri ca argintul,
> Și ochi ce strălucesc
> Ca picături de rouă pe o frunză de lotus."

7

Constructing Suitable Device for Integration of Foreign Language into Romanian

7.1. Evaluating and Establishing the Device for Integration of Foreign Language as the Specific Element of the English Vernacular

COMPREHENSION OF CULTURALLY LOADED textual units by young readers is a significant issue for translators of children and young adults' literature. Some cultural meanings are more explicit than others due to their more popular nature. Hence young reader's audience would assimilate easier names or locations than events or situations of foreign culture. The translation approach to such culturally defined units is subject of continuous debates but no research has illuminated it to the degree to provide efficient results of the actual level of comprehension of the readers. This, on the other hand, establishes the freedom of translator's choice of methodology, i.e. either foreignisation or domestication. The only guiding principle may be the need of some ex-

Constructing Suitable Device for Integration

planatory help when complex culturally defined units are in view.[1] The degree of reader's comprehension of culturally loaded textual unit of the ST is defined through the translator's presupposition of the potential knowledge of the targeted young readership.[2]

The use of foreign element to introduce the colloquial phrases of Italian and Spanish is determined by the foreign cultural elements accepted into the British culture in association with their usage in their original context, e.g. "expresso splendido" for the acknowledged Italian coffee. These expressions are known to the general readership and are used to spice up the conversation between characters giving it a distinctive character.

Dealing with the device for integration of foreign language in the TT requires a clarification of the translator's approach. The translator of children's literature should adopt a twofold approach in the process of producing the TT. On the one hand, they ought to formulate their position of dealing with the ST in regard to the use of domestication or foreignisation method and with consideration of the social, cultural and pedagogical dimensions of the ST in light of the expectations of the potential readers. On the other hand, the translator needs to take into account the diverse nature of the TT and constantly interact with the issues faced in the process of transformation and to employ an approach that can ensure consistency.[3]

A revelatory view of the textual nature of children's fiction is provided through a close analysis of its style within the influence of the genre dynamics and in the particular cultural setting. The essential discovery is that the textual strategies

---

1. E. O'Sullivan, *Comparative Children's Literature*, 94.

2. Ibid., 97.

3. I. Pascua-Febles, *Translating Cultural References: The Language of Young People in Literary Texts*, 111–12.

when grounded on the use of conversational techniques[4] within well guided narrative flow shaped by the author's perspective[5] modify preferential linguistic boundaries to allow the presence of all dimensions of the written discourse.[6] The use of the foreign expressions by Newbery can be considered as one of her strategies to stretch the reader's perception to new levels of foreign cultural encounter.

7.2. Toward Constructing the Most Suitable Device for Integration of Foreign Language to Preserve and Transmit the English Vernacular Element into Romanian

The presence of foreign words in the ST creates significant difficulty for the translator and demands specific approach in order to preserve the author's objective in the TT. The two issues which expect resolution by the translator are the intended role of the foreign words in the ST and their impact on the target audience. Lathey warns against too much use of foreign words in the translations of children literature and advises the translator to take into consideration the cultural and knowledge limitations of the child.[7] Under-

---

4. Conversational techniques include different types of speech, especially "direct speech dialogue," (p.65) defined by conversational principles and used in combination by the characters of the story and through narrator's specific guidance. John Stephens, "Analysing Texts for Children: Linguistics and Stylistics," in *Understanding Children's Literature*, ed. Peter Hunt (London: Routledge, 1999), 65, 66.

5. The so called "focalisation strategies" develop the narrative through consecutive events which shape the thinking of one specifically designated character. J. Stephens, *Analysing Texts for Children: Linguistics and Stylistics*, 64.

6. Ibid., 67.

7. Gillian Lathey, ed., *The Translation of Children's Literature: A Reader* (Clevedon: Multilingual Matters Ltd, 2006), 7.

Constructing Suitable Device for Integration

standing Lathey's concern, I would argue that the technique used should aim to preserve the original intentions of the author in the TT and facilitate their understanding by the target readers. Hence Lefevere maintains that translating foreign words is not appropriate since it may strip the text from author's original intention. Furthermore, he considers that leaving foreign words untranslated may not be enough since their meaning may not appear to be foreign to the target reader due to their language abilities. Thus, according to Lefevere, the best solution may be to make the foreign word or phrase accessible to the target reader and also offer its translation in an appropriate format within the context of the foreign word or phrase and as part of the TT.[8] A culturally defined problem of translation, according to Landers, is related to specific textual items loaded with cultural meaning which is clear for the source reader but is lost for the target audience. The cultural aspect of such items may be related to names, organisations and other culturally specific elements.[9] Therefore, I agree with Landers, that to reach a smooth transition of these cultural items, in this case the foreign expressions to the TT, one should preserve their original language and in this way rely on the surrounding context for revealing their meaning. This approach will both preserve the original meaning of the text and help the target audience to understand the meaning of these cultural items with the help of their context.[10]

Due to the fact that Romanian is a Latin based language like Italian and Spanish, the foreign words used in the conversation would be easily accepted by the young readers who

---

8. André Lefevere, *Translating Literature: Practice and Theory in a Comparative Literature Context* (New York: The Modern Language Association of America, 1992), 29.

9. C. E. Landers, *Literary Translation: A Practical Guide*, 79.

10. Ibid.

also study Italian and Spanish as foreign languages. Such words are easily recognisable by the general audience due to their exposure to Italian and even more to Colombian and Mexican soap operas in Spanish which are very popular in Romania.[11] Thus, the demand for such TV series based on Latino culture and language shows an increased appreciation of Spanish and other popular Latin-based languages such as Italian which makes the integration of the foreign expression introduced by Newbery even easier to be consumed by the younger readership. By the intense and frequent presence of these two languages in the mass media in Romania, one can conclude that Romanians are looking at Italian and Spanish as authoritative Latin-based languages which they not only accept but also demand their presence in their cultural context. In addition to the intense presence of these two languages in general, the words *expres* and *espresso* in particular are now acknowledged Romanian neologisms borrowed from Italian.[12] Such is also the case of *signoria* being acknowledged as neologism borrowed from Italian.[13]

Cultures and languages defined as authoritative play a significant role in translation as it may be observed from a

11. There were ten soup operas in Spanish noticed on the TV program for *Acasă TV* on 16 July 09. *Program TV Acasă* [TV Program—Acasă], [online], Available at http://tv.acasa.ro/program_Acasa_TV_--p4.html#A, Accessed on 16 July 2009.

12. *Cafea expres* from It. caffè espresso. Strong coffee prepared with a special machine. Elena Ciobanu, Maria Păun, Magdalena Popescu-Marin and Zizi Ștefănescu-Goangă, "Expres" [Express], in *Dicționar Român de Neologisme* [Romanian Dictionary of Neologisms], ed. Stancu Ilin (București: Floarea Darurilor și Rotech Pro, 2000), 207.

13. *Signorie*. From the It. *signoria*. A medieval government of Italian city-states run by *signore*. Elena Ciobanu, Maria Păun, Magdalena Popescu-Marin and Zizi Ștefănescu-Goangă, "Signorie" [Signorie], in *Dicționar Român de Neologisme* [Romanian Dictionary of Neologisms], ed. Stancu Ilin (București: Floarea Darurilor și Rotech Pro, 2000), 481.

Constructing Suitable Device for Integration

historical point of view. In the relationship between cultures the authoritative role is undertaken by the culture which is considered to provide a significant learning potential for the comparing culture.[14] The extreme of this position is known as "ethnocentricity."[15] The interpretative perspective of such cultures does not allow foreign elements to be understood separately from their own cultural perception. Hence translations defined by ethnocentricity eradicate the TT from the cultural mores of the source culture.[16] Language of authority plays dominant role in translations by appealing to the more marginalised languages to undergo translation for the sake of demonstrating their linguistic values through a wide acceptance. An example from the history of translation may be provided with the endeavour of formalising the place of Eastern European languages among the European language family.[17]

Newbery's integration of foreign expressions as the ones presented in the extract might be comprehended as a case of intertextuality through which the author enforces such cultural orientation and makes a statement of her cultural affinities. Intertextuality in children's literature is a very dynamic concept developed on the relationship between texts, writers, readers their knowledge and language.[18] Lan-

---

14. A. Lefevere, *Translating Literature: Practice and Theory in a Comparative Literature Context*, 118.

15. Ibid., 120.

16. Ibid.

17. Ibid., 123.

18. Desmet considers that dealing with intertextual source texts may be resolved through the use of substitutions and compensations. The former is used to substitute the intertextual unit from the ST with new intertextual unit in the TT in order to preserve its contribution to the original meaning within the target context where the meaning of the original intertextual unit has been obscured for the target audience. The compensation technique is used when intertextual unit is

guage appears to be the vehicle of this relationship which positions children readers in a dependant position to the adult writers who integrate their knowledge of various texts in their writings. In this network of interactions, intertextuality receives a threefold format of textual background relations, reformulated classical texts and widespread familiar literary units. Hence children readers interpret texts through the perspective of previously obtained knowledge from various media or literary sources carrying similarity in story line and characters, simplified classical texts and familiar textual elements.[19]

7.3. Presentation of the Embodiment of the Foreign Language Element of English Vernacular through the Distinctiveness of Romanian Language of Young Adults

Having previously shown that the foreign elements such as *Espresso splendido* and *señora* are actually nowadays fully

---

incorporated into the TT in spite of its absence from the ST in order to preserve the dynamic of the message of the ST into the TT. The closeness of the intertextuality to the translation is defined through two characteristics of the process which the original texts undergo. The creation of text from various sources impacts the message of the sources due to their interactions by intensifying and deforming it. Similarly these two characteristics signify the process of translation which resurrects the ST into the target language transforming its message into this language. Mieke K. T. Desmet, "Intertextuality/Intervisuality in Translation: The Jolly Postman's Intercultural Journey from Britain to the Netherlands," in *The Translation of Children's Literature: A Reader*, ed. Gillian Lathey, *Topics in Translation* 31, eds. Susan Bassnett and Edwm Gentzler (Clevedon, UK: Multilingual Matters Ltd, 2006), 125-26.

19. Christine Wilkie, "Relating Texts: Intertextuality," in *Understanding Children's Literature*, ed. Peter Hunt (London: Routledge, 1999), 130-133.

Constructing Suitable Device for Integration

integrated as neologisms into Romanian and that the target readership is accustomed with the Latin-based languages such as Italian and Spanish, translator's decision would be established to maintain the Italian and Spanish words and expressions as they are represented in the ST. To emphasise their cultural value, the translator will maintain the italic font in these words as in the ST. This format will be applied as well to Espresso splendido which for unknown reasons, the author has decided to keep it in normal font style. In such a way the target readership can identify the load of additional cultural element which had also been embraced by the author and transmitted to the reader through the cultural English comprehension of the foreign element. The Italian and Spanish expressions, whose presence is now highlighted in the text by the difference in the font style, are going to be understood by the young readership of the Romanian translation due to their dual familiarity, as part of languages intensely present in daily media such as TV, and their incorporation into the Romanian vocabulary. Concerning the Italian cardinal numerals they present very close similarity to the Romanian ones due to their Latin-based origins and as such pose no difficulty in understanding them. To support the argument of easy comprehension of the Italian cardinal numerals by the Romanian young readership one can notice the similarities in the following examples: *una* (it)/una (ro); *duo* (it)/două (ro); *tre* (it)/trei (ro); *quattro* (it)/patru (ro), *cinque* (it)/cinci (ro). However, the Italian cardinal numerals will be maintained in my translation to match the continuity of the foreign element as shown underneath.

> El întrebase "Vrei una, ha? *Espresso splendido* pentru drăguța *señora*." Și mama zise "Asta face cafeau mai gustoasă. Cu siguranță." Apoi Mike ne-a învățat pe mine și pe Jamie să numărăm

până la zece în italiană și rosteam numerele pe când mergeam pe stradă. *Una, duo, tre, quattro, cinque* . . . Erau cuvinte frumoase de rostit.

"Da, numără în italiană, i-am spus Domnului Rose. Mike începuse să ne învețe. Știți, tatăl nostru vitreg."

"El nu-i din Italia, nu-i așa?"

"Nu, din Leighton Buzzard."

"Și Jamie a vorbit și în engleză?"

"Da! Părea cu totul în regulă."[20]

---

20. L. Newbery, *Catcall*, 44.

8

Evaluating the Functionality of the Designed Devices

8.1. Considerations of the New Tendencies Observed Among the Target Readership in Romania

FOLLOWING THE RECONSTRUCTION OF the six devices their functionality is evaluated through the perspective of the target readership. The test has been carried out by questioning a group of sixty-three young Romanian readers.[1] The questionnaire given has been designed to assess readers' capacity to identify and comprehend the English vernacular element in particular extracts which were translated using the designed devices. It was established that the young Romanian readers' background and exposure to foreign

---

1. The group consists of 63 candidates of age between 11 and 16 years old from two different backgrounds: from a village called Damiș in Transylvania and Oradea, a city in Transylvania. From the total of this group, 33 candidates were between 11 and 13 years old and 30 between 13 and 16 years old.

cultures and languages, in particular to English, was essential to fully comprehend the English vernacular element in the given extracts.

From the total of 63 young readers, 51 stated that they can speak and read English which constitutes a high proportion of the 63 candidates. This proportion of English speaking young readers from both rural and urban areas suggests that English is the most appreciated and popular foreign language among the new generations of Romanians. These results are also supported by findings of the Romanian statistics from 2007 which confirm that in the Romanian secondary schools 95 percent of the pupils study English. The average age when a Romanian child starts learning English is eight years old.[2]

The other two foreign languages proven to be popular for the candidates were French (17) and German (16). The least popular language seems to be Russian (1) which during the communist era in Romania used to be a compulsory foreign language in primary and secondary school.[3] Thus,

---

2. Elena Larion, *Studiu în Învățământul Primar: 6 din 10 elevi români vorbesc o limbă străină* [Learning in the Secondary School: Six Out of Ten Romanian Pupils Speak a Foreign Language], *Gândul*, 24 November 2008, [online], Available at http://www.gandul.info/scoala/6-din-10-elevi-romani-vorbesc-o-limba-straina.html?3934;3544789, Accessed on 28 July 2009. Chelemen also claims that 45 percent of Romanians speaks at least one foreign language. This percentage is similar to the ones from other European states. Eugen Chelemen, "Românii vorbesc limbi străine la fel ca locuitorii altor state" [Romanians Speak Foreign Languages As Well As the Inhabitants of Other European States], *Adevărul*, 2 February 2005, [online], Available at http://www.adevarul.ro/articole/2005/romanii-vorbesc-limbi-straine-la-fel-ca-locuitorii-altor-state.html, Accessed on 28 July 2009.

3. A similar percentage was reported by Larion, 1,9 percent. E. Larion, *Studiu în Învățământul Primar: 6 din 10 elevi români vorbesc o limbă străină* [Learning in the Secondary School: Six Out of Ten Romanian Pupils Speak a Foreign Language], [online].

Evaluating the Functionality of the Designed Devices

one can conclude that in the last two decades Romanian young generations have taken a different approach toward foreign languages and cultures and have totally shifted their direction moving away from the East with Russian as the dominant language and its representative cultural characteristics toward the West, acknowledging English as the dominant language and English culture as accompanying its widespread influence.

8.2. The Efficiency of the Designed Language Devices in Preserving the English Vernacular

The questionnaire had been designed to test the efficiency of the language devices in preserving the English vernacular through assessing the comprehension of particular English cultural elements transmitted into the Romanian translation of *Catcall*. Therefore, if their presence is identified as belonging to the English culture the translator would be satisfied that the already designed language devices are successfully implemented into the TT and that they support the transfer of the vernacular element in the shape and with the particularities described in the chapter that dealt with each particular device.

To visualise the comprehension of the English vernacular elements in the two extracts administrated to the group being examined the translator is looking at particular referential English elements and how their presence was acknowledged by the readers in the Romanian translation. When asked whether the presence of the word *gugălit* in the first extract made them think of a popular Internet search engine, 37 candidates stated that they thought of either "Google" or "Google.ro." In the first extract a list of six types of psychology was also introduced from which only few are actively used in the Romanian context. However, 40 of the candidates stated that they were aware of all these types of psychology which may suggest that they have already met all the terms in other English texts or they may have heard of them in the media. The term *consiliere psihologică* "counselling psychology" was the most known term (12 candidates) followed by *psihologia sănătății* "health psychology" known by six of the candidates. *Psihologia clinică* "clinical psychology" and *psihologia legală* "forensic psychology" were known only by one candidate each.

When faced with the issue of identifying the country from which characters with names like *Rick, Bex, Domnul O'Shea, Doamna Cartwright* may have come from, 36 Romanian young readers stated that they may have come from England and 11 stated that they thought the characters mentioned above could have come from America. This represents a high proportion of the total of 63 candidates, which may suggest that most of the young readers have easily found cultural clues in the names of the characters. Even though 11 of the candidates stated that they thought the characters were coming from America that may be an effect of the limited text to which they had access and therefore were not aware of all the cultural devices used throughout the book. In other words, the translator suggests that if these 11 candidates could have had access to more extensive extracts which could have incorporated the use of all six devices developed for achieving the translation of *Catcall* into Romanian, then they could easily define the characters as of English origins rather than American. However, this would not have been practical since due to the age of the candidates, between 11 and 16 years old, their concentration span would not have allowed longer exposure to more texts. In addition, the translator wanted to encourage more active participation with a rather limited number of extracts, two in the present case.

Evaluating the Functionality of the Designed Devices

The candidates were also required to read the translation of the extract which incorporated the reported incident of Josh being told off by Mr. O'Shea, his teacher, and asked to confirm whether they would have reported the incident in the same manner if they were Josh. From the entire group, 49 of the candidates stated that they would have retold the incident in the same manner and 14 stated that they would have retold the incident in a different way. Their proposals included sentences as the followings: *Mi s-a întâmplat un mic incident la școală;* "I have been involved in an insignificant incident in the school."; *Îmi cer iertare pentru cele întâmplate*; "I apologise for what had happened"; *N-o să se mai întâmple niciodată* "It will never happen again." and *Vă rog să mă lăsați în pace.* "Please leave me alone." After analysing these results and suggestions, the translator may conclude that generally the young Romanian readership seems comfortable with the meticulous description of unhappy incidents such as being told off by one's teacher and that they can appreciate the humour included in such passages. However, there are a small number of candidates who seemed to feel uncomfortable with making fun of unhappy events such as the one mentioned earlier and suggested that a concise and apologetic sentence, like the ones mention above would be enough in order to retell such incidents.

Finally, 41 candidates stated that they thought the given extracts were taken from a translated book, 17 stated that they were not sure whether the extracts were taken from a translated book or an indigenous Romanian book, and three stated that they thought the extracts were part of a Romanian book. Considering that the overall intention of the translator was to transmit the English vernacular to the Romanian young readership, these results are satisfactory and reflect the constant attempt of the translator to maintain these elements in their best representation into

Romanian. It also proves that the designed language devices used to translate *Catcall* were successfully developed and implemented by the translator and therefore helped to effectively identify, transmit and maintain the characteristics of English cultural element throughout the translation.

Conclusion

THROUGHOUT THE PRESENT RESEARCH the translator had demonstrated that the unique English vernacular can be maintained, reconstructed and implemented into the Romanian translation of *Catcall*. This was achieved by designing and implementing six suitable devices, namely, an imagery device, reported language device, facts and data device, word play device, web page device and a foreign language device. The translator had properly identified and presented the difficulties that each device had to deal with in order to be functional in Romanian. The attempt to reconstruct each one of the six devices into Romanian was tackled step by step by the translator considering the substantial structural and cultural implications for both cultures. The representation of how each device had contributed toward the proper incorporation of the English vernacular element into Romanian was conducted in a suitable and careful manner taking into account relevant opinions and approaches of representative scholarly debates for the device in question.

The efficiency of the above mentioned devices was tested by administering two extracts of the translation to a group of Romanian young readers. Both extracts illustrate the implementation of two of the devices in the Romanian translation. The results of the questionnaire which was distributed with the two extracts had proven that a high proportion of the questioned group had easily identified the English vernacular element in the translation, and that most of the candidates had identified that the particular extracts were part of a Romanian translation of an English novel.

Due to the fact that the designed devices had proved helpful for the successful transfer and implementation of the English vernacular in the Romanian translation of *Catcall*, these devices can now be suggested as models and guidance to be followed by other Romanian translators of English fiction for young readers. The Romanian translators may find useful to have a model to refer to when making their choices in regard to the particular cultural references whose transfer into Romanian could be easily lost or distorted due to the significant cultural differences and structural textual issues.

The next step in order to test the efficiency of the designed devices as models and guidance for other Romanian translators of English literature for children could be achieved by the initiative of another Romanian translator to use them in their own translation. Alternatively, the present translator would make use of these devices in another translation from English into Romanian. The translator has also made plans for a test of the reverse use of the devices through translating a Romanian narrative into English during which process the devices' reverse efficiency will be tested, namely the preservation of Romanian cultural elements into the English translation.

Appendices

Cover Letter

Dear Teacher,

Thank you for agreeing to distribute my questionnaire to your class. Below you will find a short explanation of the purpose of my questionnaire and some simple instructions.

The purpose of my questionnaire is to test young readers' perception of English cultural elements in two extracts from my translation of the novel, *Catcall*, by Linda Newbery.

The questionnaire is anonymous and designed to be easy to fill in by young people in the age group 11–16. Filling it in should take no longer than 20 minutes. Please hand out a copy to each pupil in your class and after you receive them back please return them to me at the following address:

Monica Zhekov

[Undisclosed recipient]

Thank you very much for your assistance,

Monica Zhekov

Questionnaire

Dear,

Please read the two extracts and answer the questionnaire following these extracts. Please tick the boxes applicable to you and give a short answer where applicable.

Extract 1

> De îndată ce intraserăm, am gugălit *psiholog*. După ce am învățat cum să-l scriu corect, mi-a dat o listă întreagă. Era destul de complicată. Din lista asta aflasem că sunt psihologi specializați în psihologie clinică, psihologie legală, consiliere psihologică, psihologia sănătății, și chiar psihologie industrială. Erau multe articole lungi cu tot felul de cuvinte pe care nu le înțelegeam. Dar nu era nimic ca să te învețe ce să faci dacă deodată fratele tău nu mai vorbește.

Apoi în cele din urmă aflasem ceva care explica ce *este* psihologia, și la urmă părea destul de simplu:

Questionnaire

Ce Este Psihologia?

Psihologia este o profesie care are ca bază ştiinţa. Este studiul despre oameni: cum gândesc aceştia, cum acţionează, reacţionează sau interacţionează. Se preocupă de toate aspectele de comportament şi gândire, simţăminte şi motivaţia care stă la baza unui asemenea comportament.

Extract 2

Şi, desigur, acela fuse momentul în care Domnul O'Shea deshisese uşa. Încremenise, se uitase la mine, şi ne spusese la amândoi să mergem înăuntru.

Rezultatul: surzirea urechilor la maxim de către Rick, împreună cu clătinări dezaprobatoare din cap, şi *ruşine totală, şi sunt şocat să aud de un asemenea comportament*, şi o ameninţare cu sunatul părinţilor dacă ceva de genul acesta se va întâmpla din nou, *şi* reţinere în clasă pentru amândoi în timpul pauzei de masă. Aceasta a ţinut toată pauza, aşa că întârziaserăm la ora de istorie, aşa că trebuiserăm să explicăm Doamnei Cartwright în timp ce Bex chichotise.

1. Your age is: 11–13 ☐ 13–16 ☐

2. Can you speak one or more foreign languages? Yes ☐ No ☐

3. Can you read one or more foreign language? Yes ☐ No ☐

4. If you answered yes to the previous question please state which foreign language or languages

Questionnaire

5. Does the presence of the word 'gugălit' in the first extract make you think of using a popular Internet search engine?
   Yes ☐ No ☐

   (If your answer is no, please go to question 7)

6. If you answered yes, which one is that?
   _____

7. Before reading the first extract were you aware that there is such of variety of psychologists?
   Yes ☐ No ☐

   (If you answered yes, please go to question 9)

8. If you answered no please state the types of psychologists that you knew of before reading the first extract?
   _____

9. The following names occur in the second extract: 'Rick, Bex, Domnul O'Shea, Doamna Cartwright'. Do these names make you think that the characters are foreign?
   Yes ☐ No ☐

   (If your answer is no, please go to question 11)

10. If you answered yes, please state which country you think that they are from? _____

11. If you were to be told off by your teacher, would you report the incident in the same way as the character in the second extract?
    Yes ☐ No ☐

    (If your answer is yes, please go to question 13)

12. If you answered no to the previous question please state what words you would use _____

Questionnaire

13. After having read the two extracts, do you think that they are part of a:

    Translated book Native Romanian book I don't know

14. If you answered 'Translated book' to the previous question please state the language from which you think they were translated _____

This is the end of the questionnaire. Thank you very much for taking time to fill it in. Your answers are very valuable.

Bibliography

A inventa [To Invent]. Industrial Soft, 2009. [online]. Available at http://dictionare.com/phpdic/roen40.php?field0=a+inventa. Accessed on 16 July 2009.

Aixela, Javier Franco. "Culture-Specific Items in Translation." In *Translation, Power, Subversion*. Edited by Roman Alvarez and M. Carmen-Africa Vidal. *Topics in Translation* 8. Edited by Susan Bassnett and André Lefevere. 52–78. Clevedon, UK: Multilingual Matters Ltd, 1996.

Applebaum, Noga. "Electronic Texts and Adolescent Agency: Computers and the Internet in Contemporary Children's Fiction." In *Modern Children's Literature: An Introduction*. Edited by Kimberley Reynolds. 250–262. New York: Palgrave Macmillan, 2005.

Attardo, Salvatore. "Translation and Humour: An Approach Based on the General Theory of Verbal Humour (GTVH)." *The Translator: Studies in Intercultural Communication* 8/2 (November 2002): 173–94.

Baker, Mona. *In Other Words: A Coursebook on Translation*. London: Routledge, 1992; reprint, 1994 and 1995.

Berea-Găgeanu, Elena, Doina Moigrădeanu, Florin D. Popescu și Cezar Tabarcea. *Limba Română: Manual pentru clasele a IX-a și a X-a* [Romanian Language: Handbook for the 1st and 2nd Year Secondary School Pupils]. București: Editura Didactică și Pedagogică, R.A, 1998.

Boase-Beier, Jean and Michael Holman, eds. *The Practices of Literary Translation: Constraints and Creativity*. Manchester, UK: St. Jerome Publishing, 1999.

Bibliography

British National Corpus. [online]. Available at http://sara.natcorp.ox.ac.uk/cgi-bin/saraWeb?qy=bridging+loan&mysubmit=Go. Accessed on 20 May 2009.

Catcall (Synopsis). [online]. Available at http://www.lindanewbery.co.uk/midyearsfic.html. Accessed on 20 September 2007.

Chelemen, Eugen. "Românii vorbesc limbi străine la fel ca locuitorii altor state" [Romanians Speak Foreign Languages As Well As the Inhabitants of Other European States]. *Adevărul*, 2 February 2005. [online]. Available at http://www.adevarul.ro/articole/2005/romanii-vorbesc-limbi-straine-la-fel-ca-locuitorii-altor-state.html. Accessed on 28 July 2009.

Ciobanu, Elena, Maria Păun, Magdalena Popescu-Marin and Zizi Ștefănescu-Goangă, "Expres" [Express]. In *Dicționar Român de Neologisme* [Romanian Dictionary of Neologisms]. Edited by Stancu Ilin. 207. București: Floarea Darurilor și Rotech Pro, 2000.

———. "Signorie" [Signorie]. In *Dicționar Român de Neologisme* [Romanian Dictionary of Neologisms]. Edited by Stancu Ilin. 481. București: Floarea Darurilor și Rotech Pro, 2000.

Cobley, Paul. *Narrative: The New Critical Idiom*. London: Routledge, 2001; reprint, 2003.

Cohen, Gillian. "Visual Imagery in Thought." *New Literary History* 7/3. Thinking in the Arts, Sciences, and Literature (Spring 1976): 513–23. [online]. Available at: http://www.jstor.org/stable/468560. Accessed on 05 July 2009.

Corpuseye: Romanian Business Corpus. [online]. Available at http://corp.hum.sdu.dk/cqp.ro.html. Accessed on 20 May 2009.

Cotswold Wildlife Park. [online]. Available at http://www.cotswoldwildlifepark.co.uk/index.php. Accessed on 15 July 2009.

Credit Punte BCR [Bridging Loan BCR]. [online]. Available at http://www.cauta-imobiliare.ro/articole/credit-punte-extra-bcr.html. Accessed on 20 May 2009.

Desmet, Mieke K. T. "Intertextuality/Intervisuality in Translation: The Jolly Postman's Intercultural Journey from Britain to the Netherlands." In *The Translation of Children's Literature: A Reader*. Edited by Gillian Lathey, *Topics in Translation* 31. Edited by Susan Bassnett and Edwm Gentzler. 122–33. Clevedon, UK: Multilingual Matters Ltd, 2006.

Desmidt, Isabelle. "A Prototypical Approach within Descriptive Translation Studies? Colliding Norms in Translated Children's Literature." In *Children's Literature in Translation: Challenges and Strategies*. Edited by Jan Van Coillie & Walter P. Verschueren. 79–96. Manchester, UK: St. Jerome Publishing, 2006.

Bibliography

Gambier, Yves and Henrik Gottlieb, eds. *(Multi) Media Translation: Concepts, Practices, and Research*. Benjamins Translation Library. Edited by Yves Gambier and Henrik Gottlieb. Vol. 34. Amsterdam/Philadelphia: John Benjamins Publishing Company, 2001.

Goethals, Gregor. "Images of Translation." In *(Multi) Media Translation: Concepts, Practices, and Research*. Translation Library. Vol.35. Edited by Yves Gambier and Henrik Gottlieb Benjamins. 45–50. Amsterdam/Philadelphia: John Benjamins Publishing Company, 2001.

Google Translate. [online]. Available at http://translate.google.com/#. Accessed on 20 July 2009.

Green, Timothy D., Abbie Brown, LeAnne Robinson. *Making the Most of the Web in Your Classroom: A Teacher's Guide to Blogs, Podcasts, Wikis, Pages, and Sites*. Thousand Oaks: Corwin Press, 2008.

Halliday, M. A. K. and C. M. I. M. Matthiessen. *An Introduction to Functional Grammar*. 3rd ed. London: Arnold, 2004.

Hunt, Peter. *An Introduction to Children's Literature*. Oxford: Oxford University Press, 1994.

Images from the Microsoft Word 2003 clipboard. Microsoft Office Word 2003. Part of Microsoft Office Professional Edition 2003. Microsoft Corporation, 2003.

International Baccalaureate Organization. *Middle Years Programme at a Glance: What is the Middle Years Programme?* [online]. Available at http://www.ibo.org/myp/. Accessed on 12 December 2007.

Knowles, Murray and Kirsten Malmkjaer. *Language and Control in Children's Literature*. London: Routledge, 1996.

Landers, Clifford E. *Literary Translation: A Practical Guide*. Topics in Translation. Edited by Geoffrey Samuelsson-Brown. Vol. 22. Clevedon, UK: Multilingual Matters Ltd, 2001.

Larion, Elena. *Studiu în Învățământul Primar: 6 din 10 elevi români vorbesc o limbă străină* [Learning in the Secondary School: Six Out of Ten Romanian Pupils Speak a Foreign Language]. *Gândul*, 24 November 2008. [online]. Available at http://www.gandul.info/scoala/6-din-10-elevi-romani-vorbesc-o-limba-straina.html?3934;3544789. Accessed on 28 July 2009.

Lathey, Gillian, ed. *The Translation of Children's Literature: A Reader*. Clevedon: Multilingual Matters Ltd, 2006.

Lefevere, André. *Translating Literature: Practice and Theory in a Comparative Literature Context*. New York: The Modern Language Association of America, 1992.

Bibliography

Leppihalme, Ritva. "Caught in the Frame: A Target-Culture Viewpoint on Allusive Wordplay." *The Translator* 2/2 (November 1996): 199–218.

Lewis, David. "The Constructedness of Texts: Picture Books and the Metafictive." In *Only Connect: Readings on Children's Literature*. 3rd ed. Edited by Sheila Egoff, Gordon Stubbs, Ralph Ashley and Wendy Sutton. 259–75. Oxford: Oxford University Press, 1996.

Lukens, Rebecca J. *A Critical Handbook of Children's Literature*. 6th ed. Harlow, England: Longman, 1999.

Malmkjaer, Kirsten. *Linguistics and the Language of Translation*. Edinburg: Edinburg University Press, 2005; reprint, 2007.

Marino, Adrian. *Pentru Europa: Integrarea României; Aspecte Ideologice și Culturale* [For Europe: The Integration of Romania; Ideological and Cultural Aspects]. Colecția Plural. Iași: Polirom, 1995.

McCallum, Robyn. "Very Advanced Texts: Metafictions and Experimental Work." In *Understanding Children's Literature*. Edited by Peter Hunt. 138–50. London: Routledge, 1999.

McLeish, Kenneth. "Translating Comedy." In *Stages of Translation*. Edited by David Johnston. 153–60. Bristol: The Longdunn Press Ltd., 1996.

"Mega." In *Oxford Talking Dictionary*. CD-ROM. Learning Company Properties Inc., 1998.

Moss, Geoff. "Metafiction, Illustration, and the Poetics of Children's Literature." In *Literature for Children: Contemporary Criticism*. Edited by Peter Hunt. 44–66. London: Routledge, 1992; reprint, 2003.

Neubert, Albrecht and Gregory M. Shreve. *Translation as Text*. Translation Studies. Edited by Albrecht Neubert, Gert Jager and Gregory M. Shreve. Kent, Ohio: The Kent State University Press, 1992.

Newbery, Linda. *Catcall (website dedicated to the book)*, October 2006; updated May 2007 to include readers' contribution. [online]. Available at http://www.lindanewbery.co.uk/catcall.html. Accessed on 20 September 2007.

Newbery, Linda. *Catcall*. London: Orion Children's Books, 2006; reprint, 2007.

Newmark, Peter. *Paragraphs on Translation*. Topics in Translation 1. Clevedon, UK: Multilingual Matters Ltd, 1993.

Nida, Eugene A. and Charles R. Taber. *The Theory and Practice of Translation*. Helps for Translators Prepared under the Auspices of the United Bible Societies. Vol.VIII. Leiden, The Netherlands: E. J. Brill, 1969; second reprint, 1982.

Bibliography

Nodelman, Perry. "Decoding the Images: Illustration and Picture Books." In *Understanding Children's Literature*. Edited by Peter Hunt. 69-80. London: Routledge, 1999.

O'Connell, Eithne. "Translating for Children." In *Word, Text, Translation: Liber Amicorum for Peter Newmark*. Edited by Gunilla Anderman and Margaret Rogers. 208-16. Clevedon: Multilingual Matters Ltd, 1999.

O'Sullivan, Emer. "Translating Pictures." In *The Translation of Children's Literature: A Reader*. Edited by Gillian Lathey. *Topics in Translation* 31. Edited by Susan Bassnett and Edwm Gentzler. 113-21. Clevedon, UK: Multilingual Matters Ltd, 2006.

———. *Comparative Children's Literature*. Translated by Anthea Bell. London: Routledge, 2005.

Oittinen, Riitta. "No Innocent Act: On the Ethics of Translating for Children." In *Children's Literature in Translation: Challenges and Strategies*. Edited by Jan Van Coillie & Walter P. Verschueren. 35-46. Manchester, UK: St. Jerome Publishing, 2006.

———. *Translating for Children*. Children's Literature and Culture. Edited by Jack Zipes. V.11. London: Garland Publishing, Inc., 2000.

Oradea Zoo. [online]. Available at http://www.zooradea.ro/index.php?s=&id_fm=&lang=en. Accessed on 14 July 2009.

Pascua-Febles, Isabel. "Translating Cultural References: The Language of Young People in Literary Texts." In *Children's Literature in Translation: Challenges and Strategies*. Edited by Jan Van Coillie & Walter P. Verschueren. 111-22. Manchester, UK: St. Jerome Publishing, 2006.

"Pitulicea" [Wren]. *DEX online: Dicționare explicative ale limbii române* [DEX online: Explanatory Dictionaries of the Romanian Language]. [online]. Available at http://www.dictionare.com/phpdic/dex.php?fieldo=pitulice. Accessed on 16 July 2009.

Program TV Acasă [TV Program—Acasă]. [online]. Available at http://tv.acasa.ro/program_Acasa_TV_--p4.html#A. Accessed on 16 July 2009.

Puurtinen, Tiina. *Linguistic Acceptability in Translated Children's Literature*. University of Joensuu Publications in the Humanities 15. Edited by Sonja Tirkkonen-Condit. Joensuu: University of Joensuu, 1995.

Read, Allen Walker. "Dreamed Words: Their Implications for Linguistic Theory." *American Speech* 44/2 (May 1969): 118-28. [online]. Available at http://www.jstor.org/stable/455101, Accessed on 5 July 2009.

Bibliography

Rosetti, Alexandru. *Istoria limbii române: Limbile slave meridionale* [The History of Romanian Language: The Slavic Meridional Languages]. Vol.3. Sec.VI–XII. București: Editura Științifică; Ediția a 5-a revizuită și adăugită, 1964.

Sala, Marius. "The History of Words: Latin Animal Names." *Pro Saeculum* 7–8 (2006): 25.

Sarland, C. "The Secret Seven vs. the Twits: Cultural Clash or Cosy Combination?" *Signal* 42 (1983): 107–13. Quoted in Geoff Moss, "Metafiction, Illustration, and the Poetics of Children's Literature." In *Literature for Children: Contemporary Criticism*. Edited by Peter Hunt, 46. London: Routledge, 1992; reprint, 2003.

Shavit, Zohar. "Translation of Children's Literature." In *The Translation of Children's Literature: A Reader*. Edited by Gillian Lathey. 25–40. Clevedon: Multilingual Matters Ltd, 2006.

Stahl, John Daniel. "The Imaginative Uses of Secrecy in Children's Literature." In *Only Connect: Readings on Children's Literature*. 3rd ed. Edited by Sheila Egoff, Gordon Stubbs, Ralph Ashley and Wendy Sutton. 39–47. Oxford: Oxford University Press, 1996.

Stefanescu, D. "Children's Literature in Romania: Between Despair and Hope." In *European Children's Literature II*. Edited by P. Cotton. Kingston: Kingston University, 1998.

Stephens, John. "Analysing Texts for Children: Linguistics and Stylistics." In *Understanding Children's Literature*. Edited by Peter Hunt. 56–68. London: Routledge, 1999.

Târgu-Mureș Zoo. [online]. Available at http://www.zootirgumures.ro/. Accessed on 14 July 2009.

Timișoara Zoo. [online]. Available at http://www.zootimisoara.ro/. Accessed on 14 July 2009.

Toury, Gideon. *Descriptive Translation Studies and Beyond*. Philadelphia: John Benjamin Publishing Company, 1995.

Turner, Sarah. *Economic Concerns Sap U.K. Stocks: Broker Downgrades Hit Real Estate and Travel-and-leisure Stocks*. [online]. Available at http://www.marketwatch.com/story/economic-concerns-sap-uk-stocks-as-barclays-carnival-fallure stocks. Accessed on 13 July 2009.

Ungureanu, Cristina. *Creditul Punte* [Bridging Loan]. [online]. Available at http://www.finzoom.ro/Info/art/Advices/Creditul-PUNTE~1dcfdcda87b5467cac5ca9d67e2afa94/. Accessed on 13 July 2009.

Website device in the TL. *NetObject Fusion 7*. CD-ROM. NetObjects Inc., 2003.

Bibliography

Weissbrod, Rachel. "'Curiouser and Curiouser:' Hebrew Translations of Wordplay in Alice Adventures in Wonderland." *The Translator* 2/2 (November 1996): 219–34.

Wilkie, Christine. "Relating Texts: Intertextuality." In *Understanding Children's Literature*. Edited by Peter Hunt. 130–137. London: Routledge, 1999.

Zecheru, Ana. "Punte" [Footbridge]. In *DEX online: Dicționare explicative ale limbii române* [DEX online: Explanatory Dictionaries of the Romanian Language]. [online]. Available at http://dexonline.ro/search.php?cuv=punte. Accessed on 13 July 2009.

ZSL London Zoo. [online]. Available at http://www.zsl.org/. Accessed on 15 July 2009.